SpringerBriefs in Population Studies

Population Studies of Japan

Editor-in-Chief

Toshihiko Hara, School of Design, Sapporo City University, Sapporo, Hokkaido, Japan

Series Editors

Shinji Anzo, Tokyo, Japan
Hisakazu Kato, Tokyo, Japan
Noriko Tsuya, Tokyo, Japan
Toru Suzuki, Tokyo, Japan
Kohei Wada, Tokyo, Japan
Hisashi Inaba, Tokyo, Japan
Minato Nakazawa, Kobe, Japan
Jim Raymo, Madison, USA
Ryuichi Kaneko, Tokyo, Japan
Satomi Kurosu, Chiba, Japan
Reiko Hayashi, Tokyo, Japan
Hiroshi Kojima, Tokyo, Japan
Takashi Inoue, Tokyo, Japan

The world population is expected to expand by 39.4% to 9.6 billion in 2060 (UN World Population Prospects, revised 2010). Meanwhile, Japan is expected to see its population contract by nearly one third to 86.7 million, and its proportion of the elderly (65 years of age and over) will account for no less than 39.9% (National Institute of Population and Social Security Research in Japan, Population Projections for Japan 2012). Japan has entered the post-demographic transitional phase and will be the fastest-shrinking country in the world, followed by former Eastern bloc nations, leading other Asian countries that are experiencing drastic changes.

A declining population that is rapidly aging impacts a country's economic growth, labor market, pensions, taxation, health care, and housing. The social structure and geographical distribution in the country will drastically change, and short-term as well as long-term solutions for economic and social consequences of this trend will be required.

This series aims to draw attention to Japan's entering the post-demographic transition phase and to present cutting-edge research in Japanese population studies. It will include compact monographs under the editorial supervision of the Population Association of Japan (PAJ).

The PAJ was established in 1948 and organizes researchers with a wide range of interests in population studies of Japan. The major fields are (1) population structure and aging; (2) migration, urbanization, and distribution; (3) fertility; (4) mortality and morbidity; (5) nuptiality, family, and households; (6) labor force and unemployment; (7) population projection and population policy (including family planning); and (8) historical demography. Since 1978, the PAJ has been publishing the academic journal *Jinkogaku Kenkyu* (The Journal of Population Studies), in which most of the articles are written in Japanese.

Thus, the scope of this series spans the entire field of population issues in Japan, impacts on socioeconomic change, and implications for policy measures. It includes population aging, fertility and family formation, household structures, population health, mortality, human geography and regional population, and comparative studies with other countries.

This series will be of great interest to a wide range of researchers in other countries confronting a post-demographic transition stage, demographers, population geographers, sociologists, economists, political scientists, health researchers, and practitioners across a broad spectrum of social sciences.

More information about this subseries at http://www.springer.com/series/13101

Junya Tsutsui

Work and Family in Japanese Society

 Springer

Junya Tsutsui
College of Social Sciences
Ritsumeikan University
Kyoto, Japan

ISSN 2211-3215   ISSN 2211-3223 (electronic)
SpringerBriefs in Population Studies
ISSN 2198-2724   ISSN 2198-2732 (electronic)
Population Studies of Japan
ISBN 978-981-13-2495-6   ISBN 978-981-13-2496-3 (eBook)
https://doi.org/10.1007/978-981-13-2496-3

© The Author(s), under exclusive license to Springer Nature Singapore Pte Ltd. 2020
This work is subject to copyright. All rights are solely and exclusively licensed by the Publisher, whether the whole or part of the material is concerned, specifically the rights of translation, reprinting, reuse of illustrations, recitation, broadcasting, reproduction on microfilms or in any other physical way, and transmission or information storage and retrieval, electronic adaptation, computer software, or by similar or dissimilar methodology now known or hereafter developed.
The use of general descriptive names, registered names, trademarks, service marks, etc. in this publication does not imply, even in the absence of a specific statement, that such names are exempt from the relevant protective laws and regulations and therefore free for general use.
The publisher, the authors and the editors are safe to assume that the advice and information in this book are believed to be true and accurate at the date of publication. Neither the publisher nor the authors or the editors give a warranty, expressed or implied, with respect to the material contained herein or for any errors or omissions that may have been made. The publisher remains neutral with regard to jurisdictional claims in published maps and institutional affiliations.

This Springer imprint is published by the registered company Springer Nature Singapore Pte Ltd.
The registered company address is: 152 Beach Road, #21-01/04 Gateway East, Singapore 189721, Singapore

Acknowledgements

This book was supported by JSPS KAKENHI Grant Number JP25000001 (chief researcher: Sawako Shirahase), 19H00615 (chief researcher: Prof. Tokio Yasuda), and 19H01559 (chief researcher: Emiko Ochiai). I also would like to thank Prof. Toshihiko Hara for his detailed review for this book.

Contents

1 Introduction: Gender and Working Conditions in Capitalist Countries 1
   1.1 General Trends in Women's Employment in Industrialized Countries 1
   1.2 Heterogeneity Among Countries 3
   1.3 Divergent Paths After the 1970s 8
   1.4 About This Book 10
   References 11

2 Factors Influencing the Fertility Decline in Japan 13
   2.1 Fertility Decline in Postwar Japan 13
   2.2 Factors Influencing the Declining Marriage Rate 17
   2.3 Relationship Between Birthrate and Female Labor Participation 20
   References 22

3 Stagnant Women's Employment Participation in Japan 23
   3.1 Japanese Women's Labor Force Participation 23
   3.2 Theories of Female Labor Force Participation 24
   3.3 Factors Increasing Female Employment in Japan 27
   3.4 Women's Labor Force Participation and Policy Interventions 29
   References 30

4 Labor Market, Working Customs, and Women's Employment in Japan 33
   4.1 Employment and Working Customs and the Internal Labor Market 33
   4.2 The Multilayered Labor Market and Women's Employment 38
   4.3 The Unintended Results of the Equal Employment Opportunity Law 41
   References 43

5	**Work and Family in Japan from the Comparative Perspective**	45
	5.1 Welfare Regime Typology and the Life Security System in Japan...	45
	5.2 Politics of Work and Family	48
	5.3 A Possible Means of Encouraging Female Employment	50
	References	52
6	**Japan's Changing Families and Future Agenda**	53
	6.1 The Departure from the Family Patriarchy	53
	6.2 Equal Rights Between Genders Without Equal Economic Opportunities	55
	6.3 Declining Family Formations	58
	6.4 Aging and the Limits of Gendered Families	60
	References	61

Chapter 1
Introduction: Gender and Working Conditions in Capitalist Countries

Abstract In this chapter, an overview of the working lives of people in Japan is presented from a comparative perspective. Using a series of statistical descriptions, heterogeneity among capitalist countries was found in terms of working sectors and occupations of each gender. Differences became more salient after the economic crisis of the 1970s, since each country responded to it in its own way. Sweden's strategy was to maintain its generous welfare provision, which it funded through an increase in taxpayers due to the expanded participation of women in the labor force. The USA's strategy, in contrast, was deregulation and activation of a market economy. Even though the policy orientation of these two societies contrasted with each other, the consequence of women's economic activity was similar: a relatively higher number of women in the labor force compared to other countries such as Germany and Japan. In Germany, the basic strategy for responding to the shrinking economy was a labor force reduction to protect male breadwinners' employment. This strategy resulted in a persistent division of labor based on gender. In Japan, the unemployment rate did not increase as high as it did in the Western world. One of the reasons for the relatively low level of unemployment was the prevalence of the internal labor market. Large companies in Japan were able to respond to the crisis by replacing jobs within organizations or by temporarily decreasing overtime work. The internal labor market, though, worked to discourage women's employment, since it was characterized by chronically long working hours or frequent job transfers to distant places.

Keywords Heterogeneity among capitalist countries · Gender division of labor · Women's employment

1.1 General Trends in Women's Employment in Industrialized Countries

Many industrialized societies now suffer from a demographic crisis: namely, a low birthrate and an aging population (OECD 2015). Both can lead to serious problems for individuals and countries. For individuals, the implication is that one must continue working for a longer period because of the relative shortage in the working-age population and an increase in the old-age dependency ratio. On the societal level, there may be an increase in health and pension spending. Although these problems are serious and worth considering, this volume is not focused on the consequences of a low birthrate and aging; rather, it focuses on a discussion of the underlying factors associated with these issues. We can assume that numerous factors have caused the aging of society. There are obviously diverse paths to the same outcome according to societal type. The aim of this book is to inquire about the historical path of Japanese society.

Before discussing Japan's path toward becoming the country with the largest aging population in the world, it is worthwhile to describe the basic framework for social change, especially changes in work and family life in modern societies.

Most sociologists have a shared view that one of the powerful driving forces of change in work and family life has been industrialization and the subsequent generalization of employment. Before industrialization, the rate of employment was relatively low. In the premodern period, both men and women took part in working for profit, most of the time working at or near their residences. The working style was the "dual-earner" type. It was, at least, not the "male breadwinner" type.

Rapid industrialization began in eighteenth-century Britain and soon afterward in some parts of the Western world. In the initial stage of industrialization, women and children of the working class, as well as adult men, were employed and performed hard work in mills. The working conditions of those hard-working laborers were far removed from providing a "work-life balance." Most workers could not enjoy a fulfilling family life.

Partly because of socialist or union movements, the working conditions of employed workers improved gradually. In exchange for the living wage for men, women went back home to engage in housework, and children went to school. Hence, the popularization of the sexual division of labor was realized in the modern male breadwinner and female household worker model. Economic growth after World War II solidified this model. Leaders in industrialization, such as the UK, France, and the USA, experienced a typical process of "housewifization."

The common path that came after the modern type of sexual division of labor led to a new type of dual-earner households—that is, the model in which both husband and wife are employed. The economic background of this change in work and family life included the diffusion of service jobs and destabilization of male employment. The energy crisis in the 1970s and the deregulation of international capital flows triggered by the Nixon shock in 1971 led to the rapid globalization of the world's economy. Manufacturing industries, which had provided relatively stable jobs for male breadwinners, transferred to developing countries. Partly because of this hollowing out of industry, economies in advanced capitalist states experienced massive unemployment in the 1980s.

The 1980s, frequently referred to as the early stage of the postindustrial era, are regarded as the period when the male breadwinner model began to weaken in some countries. There was an increase in the number of dual-earner couples. Various programs spearheaded by the government and private firms went into effect to support this new working style.

This is just one side of the story, though. The other side of the changes of the period has garnered much less attention. A decline in the birthrate has occurred in almost all industrialized societies since the 1960s. The consequence was the subsequent change in demographic structure—that is, population aging. We have witnessed a rapid increase in longevity over the same period. Thus, the need for caregivers has increased. Furthermore, the increase in dual-earner households has generated a demand for childcare workers. This massive increase in the necessity for care workers has had two implications. It has promoted the labor force participation of women (because women are more likely to work as caregivers) and expanded the number of workers who are publicly employed. It is difficult to lower the costs of care work, as it involves a certain level of personal treatment for those in need of care. Unlike the mass production of industrial products, the mass provision of services does not necessarily lead to a price reduction. Therefore, in almost all countries, there are public care programs or public financial support for care providers.

To summarize, after the era of industrialization and housewifization, an increase in the number of service industries and aging reactivated the female labor force. This is, in varying degrees, the shared path among most societies, and the shift from the male breadwinner model to the dual-earner model has been the basic trend in many societies. This argument will be extended in Chap. 2 of this volume.

1.2 Heterogeneity Among Countries

After the 1970s, we found a remarkable divergence in the way each country responded to the crisis in that decade. The oft-expressed individual uniqueness of capitalist economies, such as "high welfare and high burden" in countries like Sweden and "low welfare and low burden" in countries like the USA, became more prominent in the postindustrial era. The peculiarity of Japanese society also became evident during this period.

Let us take a brief look at the heterogeneity among countries, using country-level macro data. Since the most remarkable change in work and family life during the postindustrial period was caused by the activation of the female labor force, the best way to begin our statistical description is to look at data regarding female labor participation. The labor force participation rate is the number of people in the labor force divided by the productive population. The labor force population includes people receiving monetary compensation for labor and people who are seeking jobs. The productive population generally includes people aged 15–64.

Figure 1.1 shows the labor force participation rates for males and females in 2016 in OECD countries. In all countries, the rate is higher for males, but the gap between the two differs by country. The vertical distance from the 45° line (dotted line) represents the gender gap. Japan is a country with a relatively large gender gap in terms of economic activity.

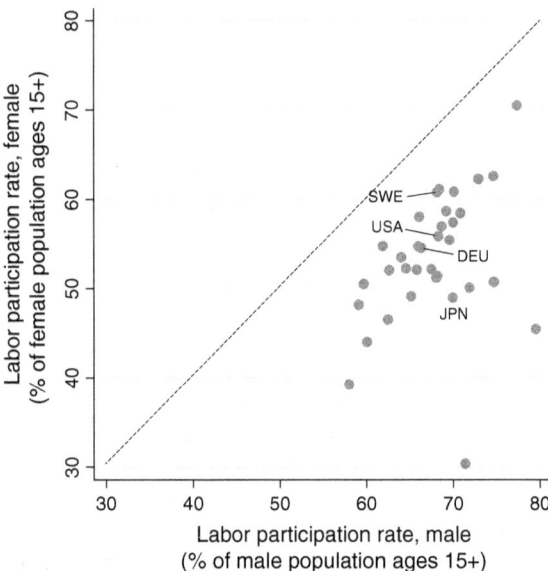

Fig. 1.1 Labor force participation rate for males and females in OECD countries (2016). *Data* World Bank, World Development Indicators

There are, however, many aspects that cannot be understood through this simple data description. First, we are unable to distinguish among various types of work. Labor force statistics clubbed vastly different working types under the same labor force category. Irrespective of whether a person works full time or once a week as a temporary worker, both are counted in the labor force.

To take a closer look at the working conditions in different countries, International Social Survey Programme (ISSP) data[1] are used in some of the following data descriptions.

Table 1.1 provides the employment statistics by gender of four selected countries. The upper table, which illustrates male employment status, shows that the self-employment rate is relatively high in Japan. In Germany, the proportions of unemployed and retired people are higher than that in the other three countries.

Looking at data on the female workforce, the differences between countries are more pronounced. Proportions of part-time employees are much higher in Japan and Germany than in the other two countries. The proportion of housewives is extremely high in Japan compared to that of other countries.

These simple descriptions are sufficient for grasping the important features of each country. Contrary to the dichotomous view that emphasizes the difference between Western and East Asian societies, Japan and Germany share important traits regarding the activities of working women. Furthermore, both countries have extremely low birthrates. These similarities are discussed later in this chapter.

---

[1]The ISSP data used here were collected from surveys conducted from 2005 to 2009. Using individual survey data instead of official statistics has apparent drawbacks, especially in terms of representativeness. Nonetheless, it has the advantage of enabling a detailed data description using individual demographic information.

1.2 Heterogeneity Among Countries

Table 1.1 Working status of selected countries (among workers aged 15–64) by gender. *Data* ISSP (2005–2009)

		Germany	Japan	Sweden	USA
Male	Full-time employment	65.1	67.2	71.5	65.6
	Part-time employment	1.5	2.8	3.4	5.2
	Self-employed	6.3	12.0	7.7	8.3
	Unemployed	9.9	3.4	4.0	5.4
	Education	6.3	9.4	7.5	2.6
	Housework	0.3	0.2	0.3	2.9
	Retired	7.5	3.4	0.9	5.2
	Other	3.1	1.6	4.7	4.8
Female	Full-time employment	38.2	37.4	65.8	54.7
	Part-time employment	14.5	14.3	9.8	9.3
	Self-employed	3.0	8.5	2.7	3.4
	Unemployed	7.8	1.7	4.8	3.1
	Education	6.2	7.1	10.8	3.7
	Housework	18.0	27.1	0.8	19.0
	Retired	7.0	1.9	0.5	3.2
	Other	5.4	2.0	4.7	3.6

As suggested in Table 1.1, the USA and Sweden are both countries with female populations that are relatively active economically. As is well known, however, the two countries have opposite features: the USA is typically characterized as "low welfare and low burden," and Sweden is just the opposite. In fact, liberal countries—such as the USA and Canada—and countries with social democracies—such as Sweden and Norway—are similar in terms of women's economic activity. In both areas, various gender gaps (labor force participation or wages) are smaller than in countries of other political persuasions, such as Germany (with its conservative regime) or some East Asian societies, such as Japan and South Korea.

Regarding other aspects of detailed work information, though, we find different features among countries with a relatively high rate of female labor force participation. Figure 1.2 shows the composition of occupational sectors for each gender. Differences by country are more pronounced in terms of women's inclusion in the occupational sector. The USA and Japan are countries with fewer female workers in the public sector. In Sweden, more than half of working women have jobs in the public sector. Usually, when people hear the term "big government," they are likely to think of a "high burden" for taxpayers. However, when we discuss work and family life, it should be noted that big government also refers to a large number of public sector workers (Gornick and Jacobs 1998). In most cases, though, a large public sector activates the women's labor force.

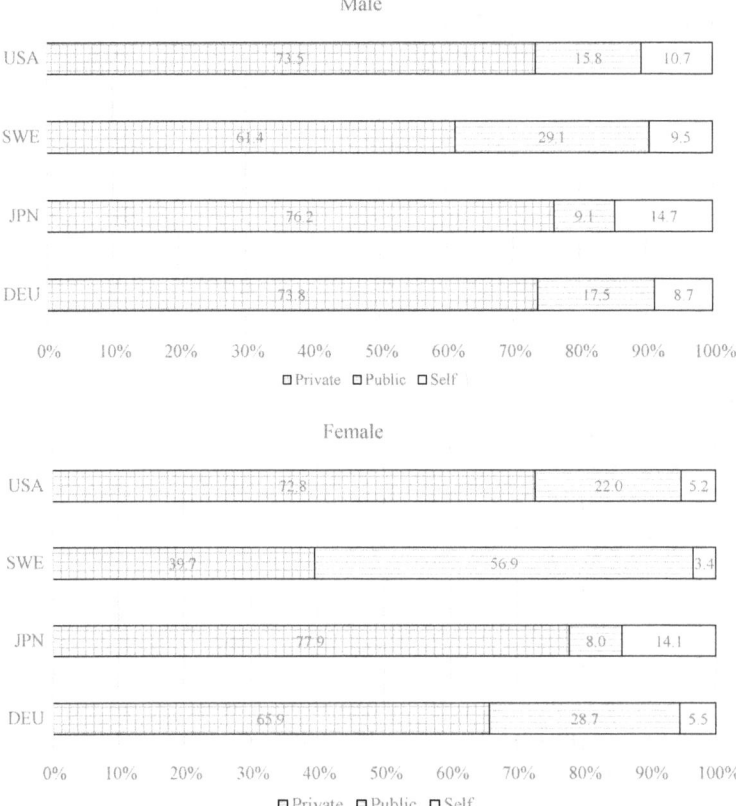

Fig. 1.2 Proportions by occupational sector (among workers aged 15–64) by gender. *Data* ISSP (2005–2009)

Let us look at a further detail regarding women's occupations. Table 1.2 shows the occupational composition of women in the private and public sectors. In private sectors, the proportion of professional jobs is higher in the USA and Sweden than in Japan and Germany, which might be a factor facilitating female economic activity in the USA and Sweden. The proportion of managerial jobs in the USA is higher than in Sweden and the other two countries. In fact, it is occasionally reported that for women in the private sector, liberal states in the USA or Canada offer more opportunities for jobs of higher rank than do countries with more generous welfare programs, such as Sweden (Mandel and Semyonov 2006).

Differences in women's occupations are more notable in the public sector. In Sweden, approximately one-third of female public sector employees are service workers, whereas the same measure for other countries is less than 10%. This high proportion of service workers among Swedish women is explained by the massive volume of public care workers there. If we look closely at this group, we find that

1.2 Heterogeneity Among Countries

Table 1.2 Proportion of women by occupation in private and public sectors (among workers aged 15–64). *Data* ISSP (2005–2009)

	Germany	Japan	Sweden	USA
Private sector				
Military service	0.0	0.0	0.0	0.4
Managerial jobs	3.0	0.5	5.7	14.6
Professional jobs	7.8	4.4	20.7	17.0
Technical jobs	23.9	15.2	21.3	17.1
Clerical jobs	22.8	30.9	17.2	19.3
Service and sales	24.2	30.5	20.3	16.4
Agricultural jobs	1.9	0.9	1.2	0.3
Skilled jobs	3.4	6.2	2.0	2.0
Unskilled jobs	13.1	11.5	11.6	12.9
Total	100.0	100.0	100.0	100.0
Public sector				
Military service	0.0	0.0	0.0	0.6
Managerial jobs	1.6	1.0	2.8	10.5
Professional jobs	28.7	27.3	27.3	42.3
Technical jobs	42.5	22.2	23.9	14.6
Clerical jobs	14.7	42.4	7.9	18.0
Service and sales	6.5	6.1	32.4	8.8
Agricultural jobs	0.2	0.0	0.4	0.0
Skilled jobs	0.9	1.0	0.5	1.5
Unskilled jobs	4.7	0.0	4.9	3.7
Total	100.0	100.0	100.0	100.0

about 70% are working in long-term care and about 20% are childcare workers. Indeed, approximately 90% of female public workers in service jobs are care workers.

How does heterogeneity of women's employment in various countries relate to birthrates? Figure 1.3 indicates the relationship between birthrates and female labor participation rates in OECD countries. Certain countries depart from this general tendency; they include Israel, Turkey, Mexico, and Iceland. As a whole, the relationship between birthrate and the female labor participation rate is positive. Detailed discussions on this relationship will be discussed in the next chapter, but one important point should be noted.

Market-oriented societies, such as the USA, and higher welfare societies, such as Sweden, both perform strongly in terms of women's economic and reproductive activity. In societies with relatively strong gender divisions, such as Germany and Japan, indicators for both female employment rate and birthrate tend to be lower.

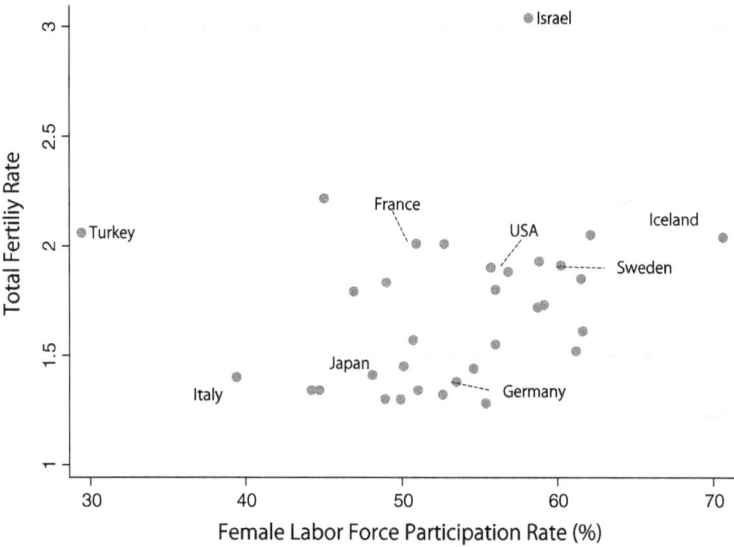

Fig. 1.3 Total fertility rate and female labor force participation rate for OECD countries, 2015. *Data* World Bank, World Development Indicators

1.3 Divergent Paths After the 1970s

One of the main questions in this book is this: what explains the divergent paths of each country after the 1970s in terms of work and family life?

Simple statistical descriptions shown above indicate clear divergent paths in each country. Again, high economic growth ended in most capitalist countries in the 1970s. A part of the differences among them can be explained as divergent consequences due to the way they responded to this crisis in the 1970s.

In Sweden, a unique economic and employment policy had been constructed by the 1960s. Under the neo-corporatist system, labor representatives and managerial groups shrunk the wage gap between companies to average levels. This wage coordination system was advantageous for firms with high productivity since they were able to decrease labor costs by holding down the wage level. On the other hand, it did not benefit low-profit firms, since they faced relatively high labor costs. In response to unemployment caused by this wage compression, public job training was provided. Furthermore, high-profit firms were expected to increase employment opportunities.

This employment strategy, however, did not work well in the 1970s. To sustain generous welfare provisions, the Swedish government undertook several strategies: one was to increase the number of workers who could pay for social security costs. In fact, women's labor force participation in Sweden had already been high. However, the increase in the female employment rate since the 1980s can be explained by the expansion of public sector workers (Esping-Andersen 1999). Women in the private sector were also able to enjoy benefits from the massive provision of care by female

1.3 Divergent Paths After the 1970s

workers in the public sector because they felt less stress balancing work and family life. These factors explain the statistics for this country (already described), pertaining to the relatively high level of females participating in the labor force and the increased employment of women as care workers in the public sector.

In the USA, in contrast, the basic strategy was to deregulate economic activities to activate market mechanisms (the so-called neoliberal route). Deregulation of the labor market had serious side effects, such as widening the income gap, but female workers did not represent the low-income group. Female workers in the USA could not enjoy benefits, such as maternity leave, from generous public support programs. Partly because leave programs were not offered, employers in the private sector were more eager to employ female workers as they did not have to be as concerned about their long absences from work. The results were a relatively higher female labor participation rate and increased activity of female workers in the private sector.

In Germany (West Germany, at that point in time), the basic response to the problem of unemployment was to reduce the size of the labor force to reserve job opportunities for the youth. The main program for attaining this objective was early retirement. Since the first priority was to secure income for male breadwinners, the gender division of labor remained relatively unchanged. This explanation conforms to the labor force and occupational statistics shown above. In Germany, the proportion of retirees is higher than in the other three countries.[2]

Regarding these three countries, similar explanations are provided by Esping-Andersen (1996), who identified three strategies: the "Scandinavian route, "neoliberal route," and "labor reduction route." The three routes are quite dissimilar from each other, but the neoliberal route and the Scandinavian route, often deemed the most antithetical, share the same consequences, as we have mentioned in this chapter—that is, a relatively more active female working population and a higher birthrate.

Now, what about Japan? Compared to Western countries, Japan had substantially lower unemployment rates in the 1970s and 1980s. Even after the 1970s energy crisis, the unemployment rate in Japan increased to at the most 2%, whereas the same figures were over 10% in many Western European countries.[3] There were at least two noteworthy reasons for this low unemployment rate.

One involved rapid and successful industrial changes. Because Japan achieved a quick industrial transformation from heavy and chemical industries to high-technology and consumer electronic industries, it maintained a relatively higher economic growth rate during the 1980s. The second reason was the unique employment system in Japan: the dominance of the internal labor market. If the demand for labor force lessens in an economic recession in an economy wherein the external

---

[2] The higher figure for retirees in Germany is also a consequence of the reunification of East and West Germany. Massive unemployment in former East Germany was countered by an active labor market policy, public employment, and an early retirement program.

[3] Allinson (2004) identifies this period in Japan as the "affluent" era. In fact, memories of the 1980s among the Japanese are usually filled with positive images, despite the reality. They include "Japan as number one," the golden age of Japanese firms, stable economic growth, the bubble economy, and the flowering of pop culture.

labor market prevails, managers decrease the number of people employed, and the dismissed labor force enters the labor market outside their original organization to find jobs. In Japan, where the logic of the internal labor market is dominant, if there are redundancies in an organization's labor force, the first step that managers take is maintaining employment through personnel relocation within the organization and a reduction in overtime work.

To some extent, this type of employment system worked well for companies' retention of employees. The biggest side effect, though, was that the system enforced a certain working style characterized by chronically long working hours, frequent personnel replacements, and occasional job transfers to distant places. All of these undermined opportunities for working women, who were more likely to have heavier family responsibilities. Thus, a stronger gender division remains in Japan, as seen in the abovementioned statistics. Japanese employment and working customs and concomitant working styles are designed for a man with a housewife. A woman with her partner cannot take part in this world unless she has her own "housewife."

1.4 About This Book

This book examines why Japanese society has been facing the problems of low birthrate and low level of women's labor force participation. Japan is now experiencing a gradual change from a society with a strong gender division of labor toward a society of dual-earner couples. However, this shift to a new standard has not proceeded as part of other Western societies, such as the USA and Sweden. The discussions of this book explore this puzzle by focusing on the structure of economy, family, and the political orientation in Japan.

This book contains six chapters. Chapter 2 explores factors of fertility decline in Japan. Japan has experienced two phases of birthrate decline: one occurred just after the baby boom in the postwar years during the early 1950s, and the second occurred after the late 1970s. The second decline led to the lowest low birthrate and caused various problems, including a shortage in the labor force. The main reason for the second birthrate decline was the decrease in marriage rate, which was caused by the marriage market mismatch.

Chapter 3 provides a basic explanation on the women's stagnant economic activity. This chapter gives a special attention on the political formation of the Japanese government. The government had designed the tax and social security systems to prefer male breadwinner families. Retaining this basic framework, it launched various programs to promote women's participation in economic activity. This chapter argues that women's relative inactiveness in working lives in Japan is partly due to this inconsistency in policy-making.

Chapter 4 focuses on the fundamental framework of Japanese employment. The employment system of large companies in Japan is explained by the internal labor market and its unique method of labor force coordination. In this system, employed people were expected to make a full commitment to their working lives. On the other hand, the employment in medium- and small-sized companies has been protected by public schemes, which has led to the survival of low-profit companies. It resulted in intensified labor. In both cases, women experienced more difficulty participating in working conditions suited to men with support from housewives.

Chapter 5 describes a total image of Japanese-style life security, using the welfare regime theory as a reference. The Japanese style of life security is characterized by its unique employment security system and concomitant welfare provisions by family members, especially women. In this chapter, it is argued that the unique life security system has functioned as a serious impediment for increasing women's labor force participation and birthrate at the same time.

Chapter 6 widens the perspective of this book by a brief historical overview of Japanese families. The Japanese family experienced the shift from typical patriarchy in the Meiji era to a modern-type gender division during the high economic growth period. The shift toward a dual-earner couple society is underway. However, problems caused by extreme aging and low marriage rates, such as care provision for people in single households, cannot be solved by the strategy of gender egalitarian corporation. A new type of social security system should be constructed to provide support for people who are unable to find informal support from family members.

References

Allinson, Gary D. 2004. *Japan's postwar history*, 2nd ed. Ithaca: Cornell University Press.
Esping-Andersen, Gøsta. 1996. After the golden age? Welfare state dilemmas in a global economy. In *Welfare states in transition*, ed. Gøsta Esping-Andersen, 1–31. Singapore: Sage Publications.
Esping-Andersen, Gøsta. 1999. *Social foundations of postindustrial economies*. Oxford: Oxford University Press.
Gornick, Janet C., and Jerry A. Jacobs. 1998. Gender, the welfare state, and public employment: A comparative study of seven industrialized countries. *American Sociological Review* 63: 688–710.
Mandel, H., and M. Semyonov. 2006. A welfare state paradox: state interventions and women's employment opportunities in 22 countries. *American Journal of Sociology* 111 (6): 1910–1949.
OECD. 2015. *Ageing: Debate the issues*. Paris: OECD Publishing.

Chapter 2
Factors Influencing the Fertility Decline in Japan

Abstract After World War II, the fertility rate in Japan declined in two phases. The first phase was the decline in the 1950s after the baby boom in the late 1940s, resulting in replacement level fertility in the 1960s. The second phase was the decline from the 1970s, which lead to below replacement level fertility in the society. The main cause of the fertility decline in Japan since the 1970s was the decreasing marriage rate. In this chapter, factors influencing the decreasing marriage rate are explored through an empirical data analysis. The main cause of the decreased marriage rate was the marriage market mismatch. An increasing number of women were obtaining high educational qualifications and were more likely to not marry men with a lower social status. On the other hand, for men, the labor market became increasingly severe. A solution to this continued mismatch problem is to increase the number of dual-earner households. However, a dual-earner lifestyle is still difficult to achieve for most people in Japan.

Keywords Japan · Fertility rate · Demographic transition · Marriage rate · Marriage market mismatch · Dual-earner household

2.1 Fertility Decline in Postwar Japan

Demographic transition is a widely observed phenomenon in fertility change wherein a society with a high birthrate and high infant mortality rate shifts to the transitional stage, which is characterized by a high birthrate and low infant mortality rate. A baby boom typically occurs in the transitional phase. Thereafter, it will shift to the last stage, which is characterized by low birthrate and low infant mortality rate (Caldwell 2004). Almost all economically developed countries have already experienced such demographic transition (Notestein 1945), and Japan is among them.

Figure 2.1 shows the long-term fertility trend in four countries. In general, there was a downtrend change in fertility; however, in the twenty-first century, it is clear that their respective fertility rates diverged from each other. The fertility rates are relatively high in the USA and Sweden but not in Germany and Japan.

The longer fertility trend for Japan can be seen in Fig. 2.2. Japan experienced a baby boom in the late 1940s, after which the birthrate sharply dropped. This sudden

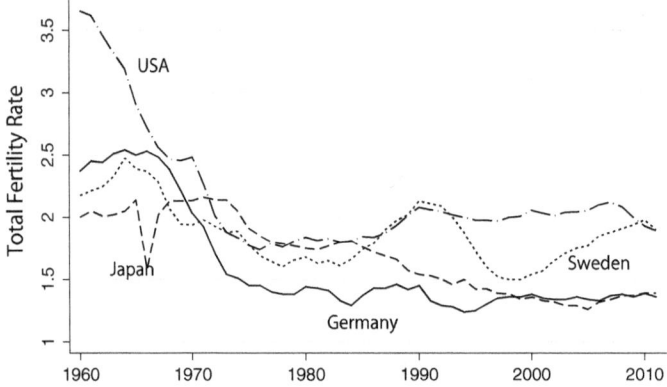

Fig. 2.1 Trend of total fertility rates in four countries (1960–2011). (There are slightly different trends in fertility in recent years. The birthrate of Germany has increased up to 1.5 in 2016, while that of the USA (1.80 in 2016) and that of Sweden (1.85 in 2016) continues to decrease. These can be partly attributed to the changes in the number of immigrants in the respective countries. In this volume, however, we do not inquire into these recent trends and factors of birthrates.) *Data* Comparative Welfare States Dataset (The Comparative Welfare States Dataset is collected and edited by David Brady, Evelyne Huber, John D. Stephens, et al. It includes statistics and indices on the welfare state and economic, institutional, political, policy, and demographic topics. Data are available for 22 rich democracies worldwide for the period 1960–2013. For details, see http://www.edac.eu/indicators_desc.cfm?v_id=50)

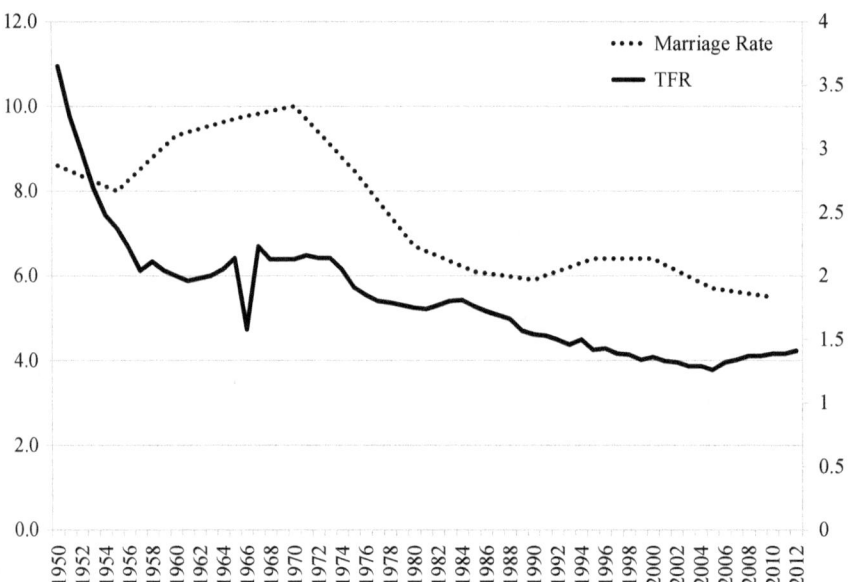

Fig. 2.2 Trends of marriage rate and total fertility rate in Japan (1947–2012). *Data* Vital Statistics in Japan

2.1 Fertility Decline in Postwar Japan

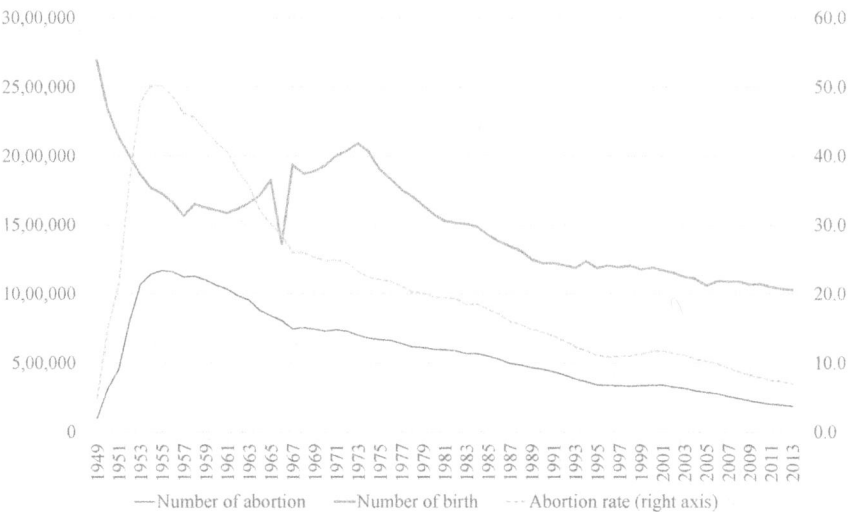

Fig. 2.3 Trends of birth and artificial abortions in Japan. *Note* Abortion rate is the number of artificial abortions per 1,000 women aged 15–49 years. *Data* The number of births is from Vital Statistics of Japan. The number of artificial abortions is from the Report on Public Health Administration and Services

decrease in birthrate in the early 1950s can be attributed to the deregulation of abortion in 1949. This resulted in the sudden increase in the number and rate of artificial abortion, as demonstrated in Fig. 2.3. More than a million pregnancies were terminated through artificial abortions every year from 1953 to 1961. However, after the stable period from the 1960s to 1970s, the birthrate began to decrease again[1]. This declining birthrate was as its lowest in 2015 (the total fertility rate (TFR) was 1.26) and then slightly increased thereafter[2].

As argued earlier, the quick drop in the early 1950s was attributed to the deregulation of abortion. However, it was also true that the average married couple at that time did not want as many children as did the previous generation. This tendency coincided with the early phase of rapid economic growth. In general, the initial phase of the declining birthrate was explained by industrialization. In a preindustrialized society, farming households may have had an incentive to have multiple

---

[1] The sudden, exceptional drop in the birthrate in 1966 was caused by "Hinoe-uma." Many people in Japan at that time believed that women born in a Hinoe-uma year would have a rough-natured personality. Even those who did not give credit to this superstition thought that the shared belief would be a serious disadvantage to the future lives of their expected children. Eventually, this deterred many pregnancies, and the total fertility rate dropped from 2.14 the previous year to 1.58. For a detailed explanation of Hinoe-uma and abortion in Japan, see Kaku (1975).

[2] For more on the fertility trend and related demographic figures in Japan, see Hara (2015).

children to maintain the labor force against the backdrop of high infant mortality.[3] During the continued industrialization, households were and are more likely to have less children, making more educational investments for each child. This change is sometimes understood as the shift from the "quantity to quality" of children (Becker and Lewis 1973).

In Japan, the fertility rate was stable and near the replacement level for a relatively short time, from the 1960s to the early 1970s. In those years, a high marriage rate was evident, and most couples had two to three children. As seen in Fig. 2.2, while the fertility rate dropped in the 1950s, crude marriage rates soared. The late 1950s to the 1960s were characterized by high marriage rates and stable birthrates. Therefore, Japanese sociologist Ochiai (1997) argues that, in this period, Japan could be characterized by the "equality of reproduction" regime. She argued that the demographic trend in Japan transitioned from the postwar stage where "not everybody married, but once they did, had many children" to the stage where "almost everybody married but had a relatively less number of children."

However, the increase in the crude marriage rate in those periods was at least partly due to the fact that the baby boomers had reached marriageable age. Marriage rates net of the changes in the age composition of population continued to decline despite the increase in crude marriage rates. According to the report by the Ministry of Health, Labour and Welfare, the total marriage rates of women born in the baby-boom period (1947–1949) were lower than those of women born in the previous years.[4]

After the short period of stability, the fertility rate began to decrease again in the last half of the 1970s. This decline, which continued until 2015, cannot be attributed to the same factors that influenced the first decline in the 1960s. Much of the fertility decline in Japan since the 1970s was due to delayed marriage. According to Iwasawa (2002), 70% of the decline between 1970 and 2000 occurred because of changes in first-marriage behavior. Once married, couples had two children on average. Therefore, in this period, there was a shift from the "equality of reproduction" regime, where almost everyone married and had two to three children, to an era characterized by an "inequality of marriage and reproduction," which comprised two groups of people. One group consisted of people who married and had children and the other of people who remained single.

The fertility rate of 1.57 in 1989 was often referred to as the "1.57 shock." The fertility rate that year was at a record low, even lower than the rate in 1966 (the Hinoe-uma year). The rate continued to decrease for nearly 15 years, after which, although late, policy-makers began emphasizing the problem of low fertility.

Many discussions and policy interventions revolved around this "abrupt" problem after the announcement of the 1.57 shock by the Ministry of Welfare in 1990. The

---

[3]Recent developments in historical demography reveal exceptional cases. In some premodern European areas, customs to control fertility, such as delaying (or canceling) marriages, were found (Hajnal 1965).

[4]See the report "Summary of the statistics on marriage (2006)" by the Ministry of Health, Labour and Welfare (https://www.mhlw.go.jp/toukei/saikin/hw/jinkou/tokusyu/konin06/index.html).

government's initial response was to expand childcare services for working mothers. The first Child-Care Leave Act was introduced in 1992. The "Angel Plan" in 1994 and "New Angel Plan" in 2000 aimed to reduce the long waiting list for enrollment in child day-care services. However, these programs did not have successful results. The birthrate decline did not stop until 2005.

The increase of the birthrate from 2006 could be partly explained by policy interventions such as the expansion of day-care services. From a demographic point of view, however, this increase is due to a tempo effect, where there was a "catching up" of childbirth by generation Y (the late marriage generation), rather than the policy effect.

While the day-care services did expand, the waiting list for the services did not shrink despite government efforts. After the bubble burst in the early 1990s, the average employee wage in Japan stagnated in the shrinking economy. The unstable employment of male breadwinners gave rise to the need for married women to earn extra income. Many women with small children were reluctant to start working again because of the shortage in these day-care services. Some returned to the workforce when the service was expanded. This was like a cat-and-mouse game. The available services were still not enough to meet the potential needs of working mothers (Maeda 2017, pp. 80–82).

Another important factor as to why the day-care expansion policy did not work was that it was mistargeted. As mentioned earlier, much of the decreasing fertility rate since the 1970s can be attributed to the decreasing marriage rate, not to the problems experienced by couples who had children. Thus, the question should be, "what caused the marriage rate to decline since the 1970s?" This is the primary question explored in this chapter.

2.2 Factors Influencing the Declining Marriage Rate

As discussed earlier, government responses to the declining birthrate were off-target, as the focus should have been on the declining marriage rate. However, arguments regarding the factors influencing the declining marriage rate have resulted in some confusion.

Most of these arguments were dichotomous: economic factors versus changing attitudes or values[5]. The former economic factor hypothesis emphasizes that the number of young people who had to face economic hardship and cannot be a part of a household is increasing. The value change hypothesis postulates that the number of people who stopped valuing marriage in their lives is increasing. Marriage has become a life choice but not a crucial one, and parental and peer pressure to marry has weakened.

However, this dichotomy is misleading when discussing the reality of marital behavior. For instance, when a woman thinks "it is better not to marry someone if

---

[5] A detailed discussion of these arguments is provided by Tsutsui (2015, pp. 36–38).

that person is not a satisfactory partner," it is difficult to categorize this reason under either dichotomous factor. In this case, she does not consider marriage as inevitable in her life. On the other hand, she does want to marry a "desirable" man, who has obtained a high educational qualification and earns a stable income. If the number of qualified men decreases because of "economic" factors such as depression, it becomes difficult for a woman to marry a man that meets her "value" criteria.

In addition, it is difficult to prove that the attitudes of the Japanese regarding marriage have fundamentally changed since the 1980s. Multiple surveys show no evidence on an increase in the number of people who have a positive idea about remaining single and not having children.

Considering these complexities, a further refined version of the theoretical framework of marital behavior is needed before examining the empirical data on factors related to late marriage. In the field of sociology, several theories of marriage are discussed in response to G. Becker's famous rational model of marriage (Becker 1973, 1974). This model emphasized the merit of specialization wherein men focus more energy on paid labor and women focus more on household labor. Oppenheimer (1988) proposed an influential theory countering this theory, which emphasizes the role of the transition to a stable work career in marriage timing. If the transition to stable work is delayed by external factors such as postindustrialization and the concomitant extension of the educational period, people will also delay their marriage until such career is achieved. When women became more involved in the labor market, the waiting period is further delayed.

In the context of Japanese family sociology, other explanations emerge. One argument emphasizes the difficulty of balancing work and family life, while another stresses a mismatch in the marriage market. "Work-life conflict" proponents argue that an increasing number of women who want to continue working face severe trade-off between family formation and work. A common policy orientation for this dilemma is to enhance support for balancing work and family.

Scholars on the other side of the dispute argue that the delay in marriage occurs because of the "mismatch" between men and women. Typically, they contend that the provision of "desirable" men decreased, making it more difficult for women to find their prospective mate in the marriage market.

The difference between the two theories should not be underestimated when considering the possible implications for practical interventions. If the mismatch theory applies, programs for balancing work and family life are insufficient to counter the delay in marriage. Women may think that they can stop working when they marry someone with a stable income. In this case, a solution is to increase the provision of men earning a stable income.

Empirical evidence indicates that the mismatch hypothesis provides a valid explanation for the declining marriage rate. Data confirming this is lacking, although circumstantial evidence does exist. The Survey on Japanese National Character has been conducted every 5 years for more than half a century. The survey includes the following question: "If you have enough money for life without having to work, are you willing to continue working?" The proportion of women answering "no" to this question has not increased since the 1970s. Therefore, it is not likely that more women are willing to work after marriage.[6]

If the mismatch hypothesis holds, the next question pertains to detailed information on the mismatch. Analyzing the data from the National Fertility Survey, Iwasawa (2013) noted that the type of marriages typical in the postwar period disappeared from 1965 to 2009. These were arranged marriages, hypergamy (marrying up) for the wife, and marriages based on the gendered division of labor.

Similarly, using the data from the National Survey of Social Stratification and Social Mobility, Tsutsui (2017) analyzed changes in marital behavior in Japan from the 1960s to 2010s. Figure 2.4 shows the distribution of marital behavior among Japanese women. Here, Japanese women with 4-year college degrees or higher are more likely to prefer high-class marriages and consistently avoid low-class marriages.

In the same period, the composition of the educational qualifications of women in Japan has also changed. More women enrolled in 4-year university programs. Additionally, in the same period, the provision of "desirable" unmarried men did not markedly increase. In sum, the marriage market from the 1960s to the 2010s in Japan comprised of an increasing number of women with higher educational qualifications who were more likely to avoid unfavorable marriages. However, the provision of

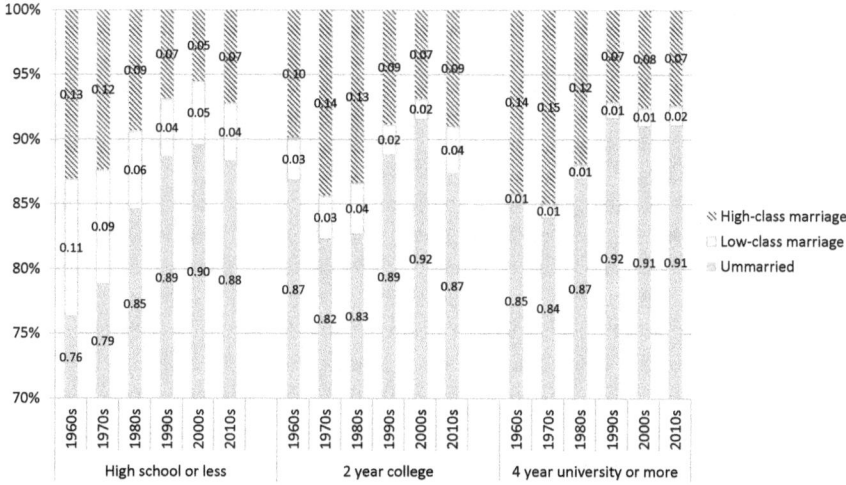

Fig. 2.4 Proportion of the marital behavior of Japanese women. (The figures indicate the probability that an unmarried woman in the beginning of the year gets married that same year. For example, 76% of unmarried women were on average estimated to remain unmarried each year in the 1960s. "Low-class marriage" means a marriage with a man with an "undesirable" job status, and "high-class marriage" means a marriage with a man with a "desirable" job status. Men with "desirable" jobs include managers, regular workers of companies with 300 employees or more, self-employed individuals with more than 10 employees, or professional workers, while men with "undesirable" jobs include those with other types of jobs.) *Data* The National Survey of Social Stratification and Social Mobility 2015 (SSM2015). The chart is an excerpt from Tsutsui (2017, p. 72).

---

[6]For a detailed discussion, see Tsutsui (2015, pp. 48–49).

favorable partners in the marriage market did not increase. This is the reality of the marriage market mismatch.

2.3 Relationship Between Birthrate and Female Labor Participation

As stated earlier, the mismatch theory was posed as a counterhypothesis to the difficulty of balancing work and family. However, from another viewpoint, these theories do not necessarily offer a counterargument. For instance, a woman facing a mismatch in the marriage market may decide to continue working to create a household and not refuse to marry a man whose income is insufficient to sustain marital life. Unless a woman consistently denies the idea of continuing her career, the "dual-earner solution" should be important to the problem of the marriage market mismatch. After all, creating a dual-earner household by promoting the policy on work-life balance may impact not only women wanting to continue their careers but also those who are not reluctant to work after marriage as a way to form a family. In other words, the two theories can be connected in how women's continuation of their careers by balancing work and life can be important in addressing the problem of household income shortage caused by the mismatch.

Unfortunately, as the empirical data indicate, the dual-earner solution has not become a major choice for women in Japan. This is supported by exploring the relationship between female economic activity and birthrate. Before elaborating on the Japanese case, we examine the comparative data below.

Figure 2.5 is a scatter diagram of the female labor force participation and total fertility rates of Organization for Economic Co-operation and Development (OECD) countries for 1971 and 2011. In 1971, the relationship between the female labor force participation and fertility rate was negative but became positive 40 years later.

The 2011 data do not necessarily confirm that the relationship between the two factors became positive and women's economic activity no longer negatively affected

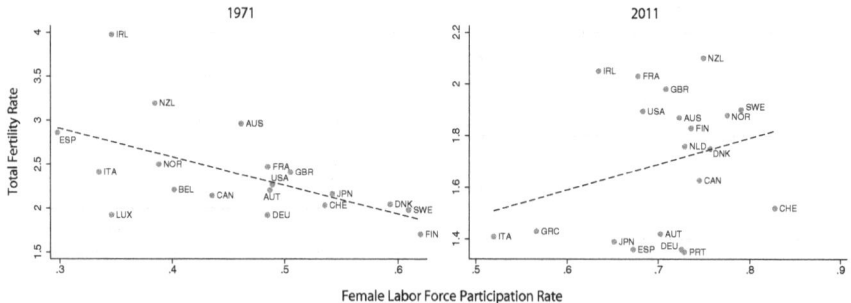

Fig. 2.5 Female labor force participation rate and total fertility rate in 1971 and 2011. *Data* Comparative Welfare States Dataset

2.3 Relationship Between Birthrate and Female Labor Participation

Fig. 2.6 Female labor force participation rate and total fertility rate in 1971 and 2011 for selected countries. *Data* Comparative Welfare States Dataset

fertility. Examining the individual data separately reveals that the "within" correlation (the correlation between values in different time period in the same country) of the two is negative for most countries. Figure 2.6 indicates individual changes for the USA, Japan, Sweden, Germany and other countries. Looking at the figures, all data show a negative shift, with the exception of Finland.

Thus, why does a seemingly positive relationship emerge in the cross-sectional comparison for 2011? There are substantive differences between countries in the extent of the negative shift. On the one hand, for some countries such as the USA and Sweden, the negative effect of female labor force participation remained moderate. However, for others, such as Germany and Japan, the negative effect was relatively strong. In countries of the former group, while a prominent increase in the number of economically active women was evident, only a minimal drop in the birthrate occurred, demonstrated in the upper right position in the chart. In countries of the latter group, an increase in the rate of working women was insignificant, although the drop in the birthrate was drastic, shown in the lower left position in the chart. Thus, the negative relationship emerges.

Yamaguchi (2008) argues that the work-life balance policy and labor market flexibility positively influenced women's continuous careers and alleviated the negative effect of female labor force participation on fertility.

The empirical data and analysis imply that certain conditions need to be met for the dual-earner solution to work, such as programs for work-life balance or labor market flexibility.

In addition to these environmental conditions, evidence confirms that women's economic activity positively affects family formation, namely, marriage and fertility. For example, Ono (2003) argues that women's income positively affects marriage in countries with weak gender division such as the USA and Sweden and negatively affects countries with strong gender division such as Japan. Fukuda (2009) demonstrates that, even in Japan, the effect of women's educational qualifications on marriage has changed from negative to positive from 1993 to 2008.

Despite indications that women's economic activity started to positively affect marriage in Japan, the influence is still small compared to other countries with a relatively high birthrate and high female labor force participation rate. Therefore, the economic activity of Japanese women remains inactive.

As indicated, the Japanese government initiated programs to enhance women's continuing careers in the 1990s. However, these programs have had only a negligible effect. Here, the question is why Japanese women have faced hardships in terms of participating in the labor market. This theme is explored in the next chapter.

References

Becker, Gary S. 1973. A theory of marriage: Part I. *Journal of Political Economy* 81: 813–46.
Becker, Gary S. 1974. A theory of social interactions. *Journal of Political Economy* 82: 1063–93.
Becker, Gary S. and H. Gregg Lewis. 1973. On the interaction between the quantity and quality of children. *Journal of Political Economy* 81 (2): 279–288.
Caldwell, John C. 2004. Demographic theory: A long view. *Population and Development Review* 30: 29–16.
Fukuda, Setsuya. 2009. Shifting economic foundation of marriage in Japan: The erosion of traditional marriage. *MPIDR working paper* 33.
Hajnal, John. 1965. European marriage patterns in perspective. In *Population in history: Essays in historical demography, general and great britain*, ed. David Victor Glass and David E. C. Eversley, 101–143. London: Edward Arnold.
Hara, Toshihiko. 2015. *A shrinking society: Post-demographic transition in Japan*. Springer.
Iwasawa, Miho. 2002. On the contribution of the changes in first marriage behavior and couples' reproductive behavior to the recent change in total fertility rate of Japan. *Journal of Population Problems* 58: 15–44 (in Japanese).
Iwasawa, Miho. 2013. An analysis of marriage decline and changes in marriage structures in Japan since the 1970s using multiple decrement life tables on first marriage. *Journal of Population Problems* 69: 1–34 (in Japanese).
Kaku, Kanae. 1975. Increased induced abortion rate in 1966, an aspect of a Japanese folk superstition. *Annals of Human Biology* 2: 111–115.
Maeda, Masako. 2017. Hoikuen Mondai [*The problem of the day-care system in Japan*]. Tokyo: Iwanami Shoten (in Japanese).
Notestein, Frank Wallace. 1945. Population: The long view. In *Food for the world*, ed. Theodore W. Schultz. Chicago University Press.
Ochiai, Emiko. 1997. *The Japanese family in transition: A sociological analysis of family change in postwar Japan*. LTCB International Library Foundation.
Ono, Hiromi. 2003. Women's economic standing, marriage timing, and cross-national contexts of gender. *Journal of Marriage and Family* 65: 275–287.
Oppenheimer, Valerie Kincade. 1988. A theory of marriage timing. *American Journal of Sociology* 94: 563–591.
Tsutsui, Junya. 2015. Shigoto to Kazoku [*Work and family*]. Tokyo: Chuo-Koron-Sha (in Japanese).
Tsutsui, Junya. 2017. Marital behavior of Japanese women since the 1960s. *SSM 2015 research papers* 2, 61–76 (in Japanese).
Yamaguchi, Kazuo. 2008. On the relationship between female labor-force participation and total fertility rate among OECD Countries: Two roles of work-family balance. In *Conference papers: American sociological association*, 1–40.

Chapter 3
Stagnant Women's Employment Participation in Japan

Abstract Women's economic activity in Japan remains relatively weak, even though it has not entered the phase of full housewifization as in other advanced Western countries such as the USA and Germany. In this chapter, this puzzle is expounded by examining the inconsistent policy orientations of the Japanese government since the postwar period. The tax and social security systems conformed to the type of household, namely, households with male breadwinners and female homemakers. Keeping these programs intact, the Japanese government launched other initiatives intended to promote female labor force participation and increase the birthrate. Partly because of this inconsistency, a substantial gender gap in terms of economic activity remains.

Keywords Japan · Women's economic activity · Tax and social security system · Gender division of labor · Politics

3.1 Japanese Women's Labor Force Participation

Esping-Andersen calls women's participation in the working world in advanced economies a "revolution" (Esping-Andersen 2009). Once considered the stable modern style of family, the model of the male breadwinner and female household worker was actually a transitional form of family in the twentieth century. He also argues that the revolution is incomplete.

From this viewpoint, the changes Japanese women are experiencing are clearly "incomplete." The gender wage gap positions Japan among the worst three of the OECD countries.[1] The proportion of full-time work is relatively low, as elaborated in Chap. 1 of this volume.

In this chapter, a puzzle is proposed. In Japan, the period when the majority of women were housewives was shorter than in some other Western capitalist societies.[2]

---

[1] According to the OECD data, the gender wage gap (the difference between the median earnings of men and women relative to the median earnings of men) in Japan is 25.7%, compared to the OECD average of 14.1%. See https://data.oecd.org/earnwage/gender-wage-gap.htm for the detail.

[2] This period roughly coinsided with the period of stable birthrate. See also the argument in Sect. 2.1 in Chap. 2 of this volume.

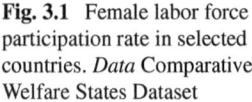

Fig. 3.1 Female labor force participation rate in selected countries. *Data* Comparative Welfare States Dataset

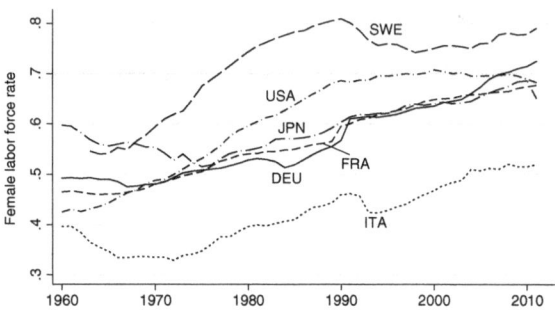

In fact, the proportion of women participating in economic activity in Japan has never been high, but also not low compared to the USA and other countries that experienced broad-scale "housewifization" in the process of industrialization. Figure 3.1 shows the long-term trends of the female labor force participation rate (FLPR) in selected countries. According to this data, the FLPR in Japan has never been lower than 50%. Those for the USA, Germany, and Italy in the 1960s were much lower than that in Japan.

However, the puzzle now emerges. Despite that housewifization in Japan is far from complete, why do Japanese women remain relatively inactive in the labor market compared to women in countries that experienced more extensive housewifization?

3.2 Theories of Female Labor Force Participation

Before exploring the puzzle presented in the previous section, we examine the basic theories of the shift in female labor force participation.

One popular theory explaining the long-term shift in female labor force participation is the U-shape hypothesis (Tam 2011; Takeuchi 2015). This hypothesis states that the FLPR starts to drop in the process of industrialization, and begins to rise again in the postindustrial stage. In an agricultural economy, both men and women engage in work for profit. The development of industrialization and subsequent economic growth, through the prevalence of firms with large-scale capital, takes men out of the household working place and into the employment, leaving women at home to do housework. In the next stage of postindustrial economics, women's participation in the labor market is reactivated. This U-shaped curve is also evident in the Japanese case, as shown in Fig. 3.1. In Japan, housewifization was observed in the 1960s and 1970s. In the USA and some European societies, it was in the early or mid-twentieth century.

What factors promote women's employment in the latter part of the U-shaped movement? To outline the theories in an orderly manner, it is useful to differentiate between "structural" and "policy" factors, which both influence female labor force participation. Here, structural factors have unintended consequences in terms of female labor force participation. For instance, the decreasing birthrate and increasing longevity are typical structural factors. Because of these changes, women were not burdened by childcare and began having more spare time in their lives after fulfilling their childcare obligations. When women raise four or five children and have a shorter lifespan of around 50 years, it is difficult for them to engage in paid work outside home.[3] However, these factors were not intended to promote female labor force participation. Nevertheless, they did have a significant positive impact on women's participation in the labor market.

On the other hand, policy factors are interventions to promote female labor force participation as an intentional outcome. These include programs such as the public provision of childcare, institutionalization of childcare leave, employment quota for women, or laws to ban employment discrimination.

Researchers who emphasize policy factors often underestimate structural factors. However, if policy factors only have effects, we cannot understand women's relatively active economic participation in the USA, because the country has almost no public interventions to enhance their working careers. In some cases, policy programs for balancing work and family are established in an ex-post manner as responses to a preceding increase in women's employment as an unintended consequence of structural factors.

What other structural factors exist other than the two stated earlier (decreasing birthrate and increasing longevity)? A popular one is the commonalization of the service industry. With the liberation of international capital flow in the post-Bretton-Woods economic regime, manufacturing industries were transferred from advanced capitalist countries to developing countries. A consequence was the prevalence of the service industry in advanced economies. The proportion of office work or sales jobs increased, which promoted women's employment.

Even in industrial economics, a rapid explosion of labor demand can stimulate women's labor force participation. In the World War II period in both the USA and Japan, women had to participate in the labor force to fill the labor supply shortage caused by the massive military mobilization of working-aged men. After World War II, vigorous export industries in Sweden attracted many working women. Most family-friendly policy interventions in Sweden were ex-post responses to this structural mobilization of women.

As indicated in the case of postwar Sweden, the relationship between industrialization and women's employment is not necessarily negative. In some cases, manufacturing industries prioritize employing women over men, mainly because it costs less to employ females. In export-oriented economies in some parts of the Asian region, it is reported that the low-cost female labor force contributes to economic growth by lowering the prices of export products (Gaddis and Klasen 2014).

Regarding demographics, aging is an important factor in female labor force participation. Aging typically occurred in the postindustrial society and stimulated a labor

---

[3] In the 1950s in Japan, a large proportion of woman had more than three children, and the average life length was approximately 65 years. The proportion of employed women was around 20% in the 1950s (Long-term Labor Statistics of Japan).

force need for care work. If a society has some level of occupational segregation by gender, most care workers will be women, and therefore, female labor participation increases.

Demographic changes (decreasing birthrate, increased longevity, aging), changes to economic structures (commonalization of office and service jobs, export-oriented economy), and an active labor demand increase female labor force participation as an unintended consequence. Certainly, policy programs have positively affected female labor force participation, as discussed in Chap. 2. Nevertheless, it is also true that afterward, policy interventions were expected to ease the conflicts between work and family life generated by the increasing participation of women in the labor market promoted by structural factors.

If structural factors do promote female labor force participation, but policy measures are not implemented to ease the conflict, one of the following two cases might occur. In one case, women become economically active, but experience severe conflicts and stresses. In the other, female labor force participation peaks before reaching the level of men's participation. Japan seems to an example of the latter case.[4] Table 3.1 shows the proportion of people in dual-earner households. Only 22.4% of the sample belongs to a dual-earner household in which both husband and wife are in regular employment.

Table 3.1 Job status of husbands and wives in Japan (2015)

		Wife				Total
		Regular employment	Irregular employment	Self-employment or family worker	Other (including homemaker)	
Husband	Regular employment	22.4	29.5	3.3	25.9	81.2
	Irregular employment	1.0	2.1	0.1	1.1	4.3
	Self-employment or family worker	2.6	3.3	3.8	2.2	11.9
	Other (including homemaker)	0.7	1.1	0.1	0.7	2.6
	Total	26.7	36.0	7.4	29.9	100.0

Note Figures are the cell-percentages of each category. The sample was men and women aged 25–49 years
Data The National Survey of Social Stratification and Social Mobility in 2015 (SSM 2015)

---

[4]One can argue that some Asian societies such as Taiwan are examples of the former case. In Taiwan, women's economic participation is relatively higher than in Japan and South Korea (Lee 2001; Brinton 2001). On the other hand, the fertility rate in Taiwan is much lower than that in Japan (in 2016, the TFR was 1.17 in Taiwan and 1.44 in Japan). The reality of the relative activeness of Taiwanese women is explored in Takeuchi and Tsutsui (2016).

3.3 Factors Increasing Female Employment in Japan

Let us now examine the essence of female labor force participation in Japan. Certainly, the proportion of women in Japan who work for money has increased over a period of nearly 40 years. Figure 3.2 shows the labor force participation rate by gender in Japan from 1973 to 2014. While the rates are quite constant for men, those for women demonstrate an upward trend. The proportion for women in 2014 was 62.7%, which is near the OECD average.

This plain statistical description has an important implication. The proportion of working women began increasing in 1977. On the other hand, a series of policy interventions were introduced afterward from the latter half of the 1980s. In 1986, the Equal Employment Opportunity Law of Men and Women was enforced to restrict discriminatory employment, job training, and promotion. In the 1990s, a package of family-friendly policy programs was implemented. Essentially, the policy interventions followed the increase in the number of working women; they did not precede it. Furthermore, what factors were underlying the increase in female labor force participation from the 1970s?

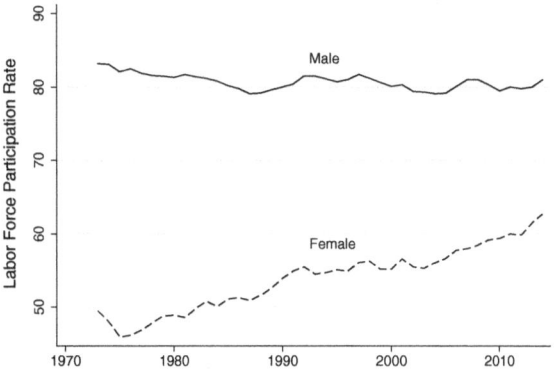

Fig. 3.2 Labor force participation rate of men and women (1973–2014). *Data* Long-term Labor Statistics of Japan

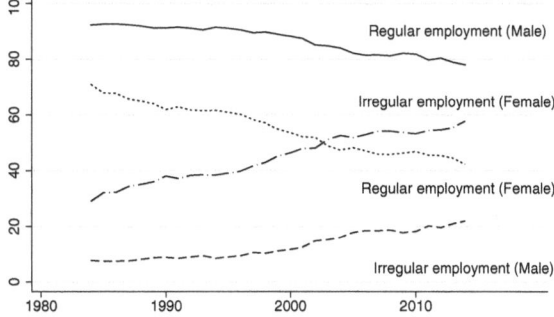

Fig. 3.3 Proportions of regular and irregular employment (1984–2014). *Note* Here, proportion means the proportion of the total number of employees. *Data* Long-term Labor Statistics of Japan

Figures 3.3 and 3.4 illustrate the employment composition. As Fig. 3.3 shows, the proportion of female regular workers is decreasing. Together with Fig. 3.4, it is understood that the number of female regular workers has been constant with occasional fluctuations. The increase in the proportion of irregular workers, especially part-time workers, largely explains the increase in female labor force participation.

Figure 3.4 also shows that the number of female regular employees increased in the 1990s. While one could attribute this increase to a series of family-friendly programs, this is not the case. From 1990 to 2000, the employment rate of women aged 25–34 years increased remarkably. Delineated according to married and unmarried women, most of the growth can be attributed to the increase in the number of unmarried working women.[5] As such, the number of female regular workers increased in the 1990s because they remained single and continued to work.

According to a government report, the increase of the employment rate from 2002 to 2012 can be attributed to the increase in the number of married women.[6] However, as Fig. 3.4 indicates, in the same period, the number of female regular workers decreased and female irregular workers (especially part-time workers) increased.

This evidence suggests that structural factors largely explain the increased female labor participation since the late 1970s, and this increase was not the intended result of policy interventions.

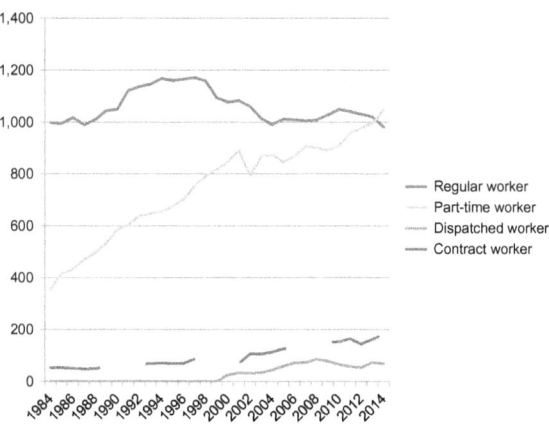

Fig. 3.4 Number of female employees by category (1984–2014). *Data* Long-term Labor Statistics of Japan

---

[5]The statistics are provided in the government report, "Current Conditions of Working Women, 2010."

[6]See the government report, "Current Conditions of Working Women, 2012."

3.4 Women's Labor Force Participation and Policy Interventions

However, some political interventions have clearly influenced female labor force participation in Japan. Two are the tax and social security systems, both of which negatively affected women's employment.

The basic framework of the Japanese income tax system is individual taxation. This system was introduced in 1950 and conformed to the "Shoup Report" published by the General Headquarters, the soccupying authority. Until then, the basic system had been household taxation.

The pure form of the individual taxation system is unfavorable to self-employment households, because they cannot deduct the wages of family employees from their household income. Consequently, self-employment households strongly opposed the individual taxation system. Upon receiving this objection from self-employment families, which constituted the majority until the 1950s, the government introduced the special allowance for family employees in 1952.

In turn, this elicited an unsatisfactory response from families wherein the husband was the only employed earner in the household. They contended that the family employee deduction system was unfair to the male earner family with a housewife, because they could not get the deduction even if a substantial portion of the husband's income was used to maintain his wife's life. Eventually, he had to pay his wife "wages." In response, the government implemented the spousal deduction system in 1961, which with occasional modifications, continues until now.

To apply for the spousal deduction, the spouse of a main earner (typically the main earner is the husband) has to restrict one's income to a certain level.[7] Some scholars and policy-makers argue that this deduction system demotivates women's participation in the labor market by penalizing extra income.

Another system that reportedly hinders women's active labor force participation is a series of social security exemption programs. Essentially, if married to an employed person, a spouse with no or a small income does not have to pay the insurance fee of the national pension plan and medical insurance plan, but holds claims for future benefits. This exemption program is one factor restraining married women's labor force participation.

Overall, there are two lines of policy interventions regarding female labor force participation in postwar Japan. One line includes the tax and social security system, which were developed from the 1960s through 1980s in favor of single-earner couples. The basic income tax system in postwar Japan is in the form favorable to dual-earner couples. However, the amendments that followed favored households with male breadwinners and female homemakers. The social pension plan and medical insurance plan also work for gender-divided households.

---

[7]From January 2018, to obtain the full tax reduction, a spouse's annual income (if there is no income other than employment income) should be less than 1,500,000 yen (approximately 14,000 US dollars).

The other line consists of the gender equal employment regulations and family-friendly programs to enhance dual-earner couples, which started in the late 1980s. These were the Equal Employment Law in 1986, Childcare Leave Act in 1992, and programs to expand public daycare for children. Keeping the "conservative" tax and social security systems intact, Japanese policy-makers introduced interventions intended to enhance female labor force participation and the birthrate at the same time.

The coexistence of these contradictory policy interventions is perhaps why Japanese women are relatively inactive in the labor market. Thus, why has this inconsistency occurred?

It is difficult to clearly answer this puzzle. However, it can be argued that the inconsistency is the essence of the Japanese welfare policy. R. Goodman and I. Peng insist that Japanese policy-makers spread their political measures in a "peripatetic" way (Goodman and Peng 1997). That is, at one time, they copied a system in the UK, and at another, they followed Germany, rather than developing programs following a consistent principle. Facing various problems, policy-makers in each period in history learned from heterogeneous societies[8] and launched programs in a makeshift manner. A typical case is the family-friendly programs developed in the 1990s. They were introduced without considering their compatibility with other systems as a quick response to the sudden recognition of the rapidly decreasing birthrate.

However, the inconsistency in policy interventions is not the only reason the economic activity of Japanese women is weak. A more important factor is the customs characterizing the private sector, in other words, the incompatibility between female employment, Japanese employment, and work-related customs. This argument is explored in the next chapter.

References

Brinton, Mary C. 2001. Married women's labor in East Asian economics. In *Women's working lives in East Asia*, ed. Mary C. Brinton, 1–37. Stanford: Stanford University Press.

Esping-Andersen, Gosta. 2009. *The incomplete revolution*. Polity Press.

Gaddis, Isis, and Stephan Klasen. 2014. Economic development, structural change, and women's labor force participation: A reexamination of the feminization U hypothesis. *Journal of Population Economics* 27: 639–681.

Goodman, Roger, and Ito Peng. 1997. The East Asian welfare states: Peripatetic learning, adaptive change, and nation-building. In *Welfare states in transition*, ed. Gosta Esping-Andersen, 192–224. Sage Publications.

Lee, Yean-Ju. 2001. Women, work, and marriage in three East Asian labor markets: The cases of Taiwan, Japan, and South Korea. In *Women's working lives in East Asia*, ed. Mary C. Brinton, 96–124. Stanford: Stanford University Press.

---

[8]In most cases, models originated in advanced Western countries such as the UK, Germany, the USA, or France. For instance, the social insurance system in Japan was built on the German model. Programs in the USA influenced postwar tax systems and the education system. Some family friendly programs such as the allowance for dependent children are similar to those in France.

Takeuchi, Maki. 2015. Toward a dynamic theory of female labor force participation: The case of Taiwan. *Ritsumeikan Social Sciences Review* 51: 73–92 (in Japanese).

Takeuchi, Maki, and Junya Tsutsui. 2016. Combining Egalitarian working lives with Traditional attitudes: Gender role attitudes in Taiwan, Japan, and Korea. *International Journal of Japanese Sociology* 25: 100–116.

Tam, Henry. 2011. U-shaped female labor participation with economic development: Some panel data evidence. *Economics Letters* 110: 140–142.

Chapter 4
Labor Market, Working Customs, and Women's Employment in Japan

Abstract In this chapter, the weak economic activity of women in Japan is explained on the basis of the country's unique employment and working customs. The Japanese type of internal labor market demands an intense commitment on the part of employees, frequently involving long working hours or even relocation to distant places at the employer's discretion. Women, who normally have heavier household and childcare responsibilities, have had difficulty conforming to this employment system. The Equal Employment Law did not have a distinct effect, because it was intended to introduce women to the working world of men without changes to employment and working customs.

Keywords Japan · Labor market · Working and employment customs · Gender equality

4.1 Employment and Working Customs and the Internal Labor Market

As was briefly stated in Chap. 1, Japanese employment and working customs have had a large impact on Japanese women's labor force participation.

In the previous chapter, I argued that the policy interventions intended to enhance female labor force participation have had virtually no positive effect. One reason for this ineffectiveness is the inconsistent policy-making that has already been illustrated. It is, however, not the only reason. Another important factor that makes it difficult for women to enter the working world is the nature of Japanese employment and working customs.

Before stating my argument on the relationship between Japanese employment and working customs and female labor force participation, let us start with a description of Japanese employment and working customs.

The established view about the Japanese employment system is that it is characterized by three features: lifetime (tenured) employment, seniority-based rewards, and enterprise unions (Haitani 1978). This classic characterization is said to go back to Abegglen's observation in the 1950s (Abegglen 1958). At this time, most intellectuals tried to explain the system in terms of an idiosyncrasy of Japanese society compared to Western societies, such as group-centered mentality or familistic management.

An updated view on the Japanese employment system, however, adopts an alternative explanation. The concept of the internal labor market became well known in a landmark monograph by Doeringer and Piore, which was mainly meant to analyze the labor market in the USA (Doeringer and Piore 1971). After the introduction of this concept in Japan, a variety of interpretations and applications of it to the Japanese employment system emerged.

The internal labor market theory has a distinct merit over the traditional view, because the three features can be explained by the theory of the internal labor market, whereas the traditional view cannot incorporate the internal labor market argument within its own framework. In other words, the internal labor market framework is more encompassing.

What is like to be an employee in the Japanese version of the internal labor market? Rather than providing a direct definition, let us start with the resulting features of it.

The most peculiar features of Japanese employment customs are the three "indeterminate" features of work (Hamaguchi 2009). They are the indeterminate type of employment, the indeterminate working hours, and the indeterminate work location. Not all employees must come to terms with these working conditions, but one is expected to accept these indeterminate features if one hopes to be promoted in an organization. That means, a person should agree to be relocated to various types of jobs, should accept a job transfer to a distant location, and should engage in chronic overtime work at the employer's discretion.

All three features of the indeterminate nature of jobs in Japanese organizations can be explained by the Japanese version of the internal labor market. The internal labor market refers to a human resource allocation system where adjustments of labor power occur within an organization.[1] The priorities of the internal labor market are an important feature, especially for large-scale organizations in Japan. This system is so popular in large organizations that many Japanese workers, when an important position becomes vacant, do not even think of recruiting a person from the outside labor market. The first thing they think of is to relocate someone from within the organization to fill the vacant position. Adjustments to the labor force within an organization naturally lead to frequent job rotations.

The job type indeterminateness is experienced like this: at the time a person is employed by a company, especially if that person is a new graduate, he or she usually does not have any information about what he or she will do at that company. Even employers or managers often do not have any idea about what type of job the new employee will perform in the company. The new employee's position is indeterminate. After the period of training and education, usually lasting for a month or two, managers finally allocate jobs to new employees. During a career in the same organization, he or she will undergo frequent job changes under the same employer.

---

[1] For a general explanation of the internal labor market, see Doeringer and Piore (1971). For the origins of internal labor markets in Japan, see Jacoby (1979) and Taira (1988).

4.1 Employment and Working Customs and the Internal Labor Market

For employers, this means that they must always think about personnel relocation within the organization. For employees, this is experienced as frequent job changes.

To illustrate, a person who is hired by a university just after graduation and starts his or her career as a clerical staff member in a faculty office may, after four or five years of service, be relocated to a public relations job in the employment division at the same university. Most of the time, the personnel relocation is a legitimate work order; therefore, denial of it may easily lead to dismissal. This system of frequent personnel relocation is prevalent in most large-scale organizations in Japan, including both large private companies and government offices. Even in medium- or small-sized firms, personnel may be subject to job relocation if the firm has various types of jobs or departments.

The indeterminate nature of jobs is the main reason that most Japanese organizations adopt a unique recruitment system. Most students get unofficial job offers (*naitei*) before graduation. Quite a few students who expect their graduation within a year get job offers before July.[2] A group of new employees (usually the newly graduated) enters the organization on the 1st of April in almost all companies, and most organizations hold an initiation ceremony similar to the enrollment ceremony in schools.

If a company prioritizes the outside labor market, it does not have hold costly training programs. All it must do is recruit necessary personnel from the outside labor market by posing the job description of a vacant position. Naturally, recruitment does not have to happen only once a year. An internal labor market, on the other hand, usually requires original and systematic on-the-job training programs, because employees are expected to hold extensive and general knowledge about the organization to which they belong in order to be placed in various positions inside the organization.

One reason that many large-scale organizations in Japan prefer the unique "one-shot" hiring system rather than year-round external recruitment can be explained by this need for a systematic training program. Companies can save on the cost of training if new employees join the company at the same time, namely, on April 1st.

The indeterminate location of work can also be explained by the Japanese version of the internal labor market. In order to adjust human resources within a company that encompasses distant workplaces, employers should not hesitate to order job transfers or relocation of employees to distant places. For a new employee, he or she usually does not know the first place of work until the end of the initial period of training. In many cases, the first place where new employees work is the central office, where

---

[2]The school year in Japan starts in April and ends in March. If students expect to graduate in March 2019, they usually hope to get at least one job offer by the early half of 2018. Of course, the probability of getting unofficial job offers depends on a student's performance on company entrance exams and on economic trends, as well as educational qualifications and the prestige of the student's school. For detailed discussions of this recruitment process, see Brinton (2010) and Fong and Tsutsui (2015).

they go through initial training for a month or two. After that, they fan out across distant places.[3]

The indeterminate working time, namely, chronic overtime, is one of the ramifications of the Japanese-style internal labor market. Because an employer must adjust labor quantity without adoption or dismissal of regular employees, adjusting the working time of present employees is the dominant measure. In order to avoid dismissals during a downturn in business, the number of employees employed when the company's performance is good should be restricted to the minimum. That is, the employer must compensate for the labor force shortage by giving an order for employees to work long hours.

Let us show some related statistics. Table 4.1 is the proportion of companies that had personnel relocations (sometimes called job rotations) in a year. The proportion is higher for larger companies. Indeed, 99.1% of companies with 5,000 or more employees had at least one relocation. Interestingly, employers enforce fewer personnel relocations for workers in technical or research jobs. This makes sense because the jobs of those workers are more fixed. It would be more difficult to relocate those technical workers to another department. For technical workers, the outside labor market is also more readily usable; hence there is relatively less internal labor market activity for them.

There is an extensive survey that demonstrates the prevalence of job transfers (indeterminate job location). Table 4.2 shows the results of this survey. The probability that an employee will get transferred depends on the company size. Employees of larger companies have a higher chance of getting transferred to a different workplace.

The survey has numerous related data on job transfers. An overall 76.4% of companies do not have written regulations on job transfers; thus most of the job transfer orders can be made at an employer's discretion. The proportion of companies, if restricted to those with more than 100 business places, 60% of whose employees

Table 4.1 Proportions (%) of companies that conducted at least one personnel relocation in a year

Firm size	Conducted personnel relocation				No personnel relocation
	Clerical job	Technical or research job	Non-clerical job	Total	
Total	28.3	19.2	35.1	47.5	52.5
5,000 or more	95.9	61.7	84.3	99.1	0.9
1,000–4,999	88.7	57.4	77.7	95.3	4.7
300–999	73.4	49.0	71.6	89.2	10.8
100–299	45.6	28.7	51.0	68.1	31.9
30–99	17.0	12.3	25.7	36.0	64.0

Data Survey on Employment Management (2002)

---

[3]Relocation to distant places is called "*tenkin*" in Japanese. Usually, the first transfer from the place of initial training is not called a *tenkin*. Instead, it is called a "*funin*."

4.1 Employment and Working Customs and the Internal Labor Market

Table 4.2 Probability of getting a job transfer by size of company

Firm size	N	Most regular workers have a chance to be transferred	Chance of getting transferred is restricted even for regular workers	Almost no chance of transfer	No answer
1,000 or more	344	50.9	27.3	14.8	7.0
500–999	460	39.8	30.2	21.5	8.5
300–499	598	31.6	28.3	27.8	12.4
299 or less	389	16.5	24.2	43.7	15.7

Data Survey on job transfer (The Japan Institute for Labour Policy and Training 2017)

have experienced job transfers, is 48.8%. Job transfers are not as frequent as personnel relocation within the same institution; nonetheless, they are not uncommon.

An important distinction must be made here. Not all employees in an organization are susceptible to the indeterminate nature of jobs. Employees who are expected to accept frequent job rotations and occasional transfers are called "*sogo-shoku*," and this is a type of employment status. *Sogo* means "comprehensive," and if a person's

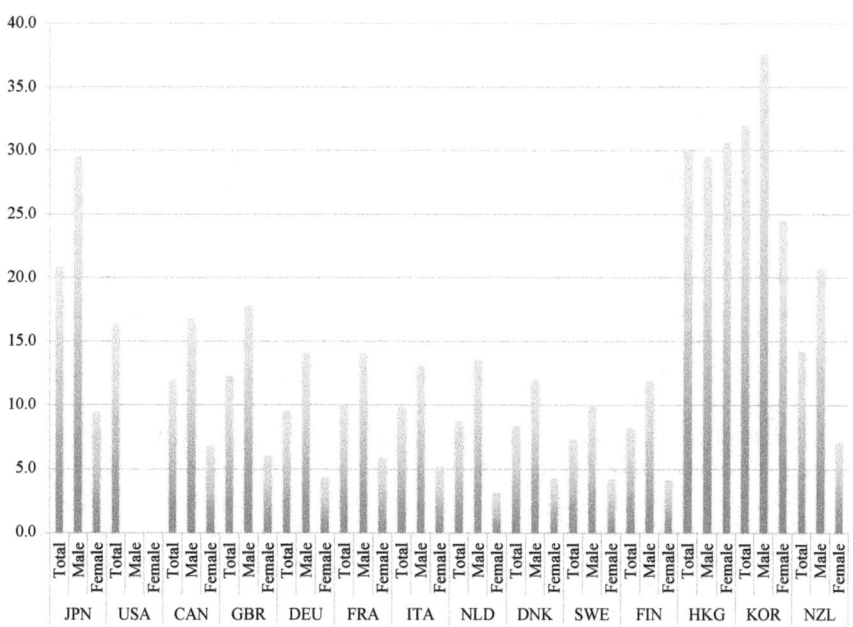

Fig. 4.1 Proportion of workers working 49 h or more per week (2015). *Note* Gender-specific data for the USA is not available. *Data* 2017 Databook of International Labor Statistics (The Japan Institute for Labour Policy and Training)

employment status is *sogo-shoku*, he or she is supposed to accept all three types of indeterminateness: job type, place of work, and working time. *Sogo-shoku* is the most common employment type of regular workers without fixed-term contracts. All other types of regular (indefinite contract term) workers can be categorized as being restricted to a determined job type.

One of the best-known features of Japanese employment is frequent overtime. Figure 4.1 provides the basic statistics regarding the proportion of overtime workers. Proportions in Japan, although smaller than those in some other East Asian countries, are higher than those in Western countries. Here, one can easily notice that the proportions of men and women differ significantly. The main reason for this difference in working hours is that their employment status is different. The "type of job" feature of the Japanese labor market is quite important when we discuss women's economic activity. This argument will be developed in the next section.

4.2 The Multilayered Labor Market and Women's Employment

Two important discussions must be added to the argument on the Japanese internal labor market, and both are closely related to women's labor force participation.

The first point is that the internal labor market in Japan, in order to be maintained, requires a buffer that is expected to absorb the labor surplus. Throughout the 1960s to 1980s, the unemployment rate of Japan was kept relatively low compared to most Western countries. Part of the reason can be explained by the flexible personnel relocation within each company: namely, the internal allocation of labor inside organizations. Other factors that contributed to absorbing the labor surplus should also be emphasized.[4]

One of these factors was the fact that the old economic sector consisted of small-sized self-employment entities. In Japan, because of the rapid economic growth, small-capital business was still active even after the high economic growth ended in the 1970s. In 1980, 19.2% of all male workers were self-employed or family workers. There was a high probability that a man who lost his job in an urban area would go back to his hometown and join his family's business.

Small family enterprises were not the only sector which absorbed the labor surplus. The other factor was that the function of the outside labor market had been working as a buffer to the employment adjustment of the internal labor market. If a labor surplus arises in a company, adjustments inside the company (personnel relocation and working time reduction) can be tried, but in many cases, an additional adjustment of irregular workers (contract employees or part-time employees) is needed.

---

[4]This view is developed by Masami Nomura, a Japanese researcher of labor. See, for instance, Nomura (1998). For an English introduction to his argument, see Mouer and Kawanishi (2005, pp. 61–62).

4.2 The Multilayered Labor Market and Women's Employment

This "secondary" labor market for irregular workers is often for low-skilled, low-wage jobs with almost no chance of getting on-the-job training and promotions (Doeringer and Piore 1971; Ohkusa 1997). Nevertheless, into at least the 1980s, dismissals of irregular workers were not likely to be serious labor disputes, because most of the irregular workers were women who were married to male breadwinners with stable incomes.

The second point is not about labor force adjustment, but about a barrier which divides different layers of the labor market. This point has been important in terms of gender equality employment policies since the 1990s. In the previous section, I argue that Japanese working customs (frequent job changes, occasional transfers, chronic overtime) are related to the Japanese style of internal labor market. In other words, employees who have less attachment to internal labor markets are not expected to accept those indeterminate features. Most of the time, those who avoid the internal labor market conditions are women, because they are more likely to have difficulty making a full commitment to them. In short, the Japanese version of the internal labor market does not get along with women's career-building.

Table 4.3 lists the types of direct employment in Japan. Those employment statuses differ not only in terms of contract terms and working hours but also in terms of the extent of flexibility (job, location, and time) a worker is supposed to accept. That is, if a worker is either *sogo-shoku* or *area-sogo-shoku*, he or she must be prepared for

Table 4.3 Types of employment in a Japanese organization

	Term	Description of job	Place of work	Working hours
Sogo-shoku	None (until compulsory retirement)	Indeterminate	Indeterminate	Full-time, with frequent overtime work
Area-sogo-shoku	None (until compulsory retirement)	Indeterminate	Restricted within certain area	Full-time, with frequent overtime work
Ippan-shoku	None, but retirement after marriage or childbirth is common	Restricted (assistance for Sogo-shoku)	Restricted within certain area (usually smaller than area-sogo-shoku)	Full-time. Overtime work is usually rare
Keiyaku-shoku	Usually 3–5 years	Restricted	Same place throughout the term	Full-time. Overtime work is usually rare
Part-time-shoku	Case by case	Restricted	Same place	Usually fewer working hours than other full-time jobs

frequent overtime work and job changes. If a worker is an *area-sogo-shoku*, he or she is exempt from transfer to distant places.[5] If a worker is an *ippan-shoku* worker, he or she is usually exempt from all three types of indeterminateness.

I wrote "he or she" to refer to an *area-sogo-shoku* worker or an *ippan-shoku* worker, but in most cases, it is a "she." In general, if an employment type becomes more restricted, it attracts more women. In fact, in all employment types other than the most unrestricted type (*sogo-shoku*), most workers are women. For instance, proportion of new female *sogo-shoku* employees was 22.2%, while for *ippan-shoku*, it was 82.1%.[6]

The employment-type spectrum by the extent of restriction has strong correlations with gender composition and wage differences. As stated, most restricted employment opportunities are occupied by women. Furthermore, if a worker accepts the unrestricted nature of the work, he or she can earn higher income.

Let us reflect briefly on Japanese employment in the 1950s. Previous arguments on the characteristics of Japanese labor markets have been developed according to the concept of the "duality" (or dualism) of the labor market. The discussion at that time was dominated by dualism regarding firm size: that is, the division of small or medium companies and large companies. This dichotomy was the most powerful factor driving the wage gap in the 1950s.

With the rapid economic growth of the 1960s, the homogenization of labor conditions commenced (Lechevalier 2017). This was the period when male breadwinner households became more prevalent. Therefore, the wage gap existed among male breadwinners, and it was shrinking. As stated, in the 1970s and 1980s, the Japanese economy was still enjoying relatively stable development. The male breadwinner model became even more prevalent during that time.

After the 1980s, when economic stagnation arose, a new type of segmentation became manifest. This time, the segmentation was between male and female employment. On the one hand, there is an internal labor market where workers accept the indeterminate nature of work and where most of the employees are men. On the other hand, there are external labor markets where more restricted conditions apply and where most of the employees are women.

The sex ratio by employment type can be readily explained by simple logic. If a person bears a lot of responsibilities in his or her private life, such as housework duties or a commitment to childcare or eldercare, he or she will have difficulty accepting the unrestricted features of work. Therefore, women in Japan have long been excluded from the internal labor market, where a worker is likely to have a good prospect of wage raises and career advancement, because they cannot accept the indeterminate conditions.

---

[5]While *area-sogo-shoku* workers are exempt from transfers to distance places, this does not mean that the worker can avoid all relocation orders. The worker may be ordered to move to different workplaces within a certain district. In most cases, an area comprises several prefectures (such as Kinki district). To illustrate, an *area-sogo-shoku* worker might be relocated from Osaka City in Osaka Prefecture to Maizuru City in Kyoto Prefecture. Usually it takes two or three hours to commute by public transportation; hence, he or she must move to the new location.

[6]Figures are from a survey on course-based human resource management systems in 2014 by the Ministry of Health, Labor and Welfare. In this case, *sogo-shoku* includes *area-sogo-shoku*.

4.3 The Unintended Results of the Equal Employment Opportunity Law

At least in the 1980s, the main reason for the gender divide in the labor market was understood to be the discriminatory attitudes of employers and bosses. This was partly true, of course, considering that large-scale companies did not employ female *sogo-shoku* workers at all. Almost all female workers in large companies did not have a choice other than a restricted *ippan-shoku* career, which was expected to end with marriage or childbirth, or part-time employment when their children grew older.

The first systematic political intervention to weaken the barrier was the Equal Employment Law implemented in 1986.[7] This legal move to restrict discriminatory employment practices was beyond doubt a landmark, considering the extremely discriminatory treatment of women in the workplace at that time. This law has been revised several times, but its main purpose remains unchanged: to prohibit or restrict gender discrimination in employment, training, and promotions.

As was suggested earlier, the effect of this intervention has been limited. Soon after the implementation of the law, most large companies made the system of "course-based human resource management" (*kosubetsu-kanri-seido*). That is, they built a division of *sogo-shoku* with unrestricted work features and *ippan-shoku* with a restricted working style.[8] The proportion of women employed as *sogo-shoku* has been small. According to a government report (White Paper on Gender Equality, by the cabinet office of Japan) from 2013, the figure was only 11.6%. The fact that employers continued to avoid female *sogo-shoku* workers can be seen as an indication of discrimination. The report went on, however, to show that among the female *sogo-shoku* workers who had started their career ten years prior, the proportion of those who had quit the job was 65.1%, more than double the rate of men. In fact, in nearly half the companies that employed female *sogo-shoku* workers ten years ago, all the female *sogo-shoku* workers had left.

What can explain this massive "flight" from the career world by women? The usual suspect continues to be gender discrimination. Based on this understanding, policymakers have incessantly added revisions to the original Equal Employment Law to close the loopholes. From the start, the initial law was often criticized as being full of loopholes. The law started with prohibitions on discrimination in training, benefits, retirement, and dismissal, and while discrimination in employment and promotions was not prohibited, employers were required to "make an effort" not to discriminate.

---

[7]The law is usually referred to as the "Equal Employment Opportunity Law between Men and Women." In this volume, the "Equal Employment Law" is used for brevity.

[8]Before the appearance of course-based human resource management, most companies allocated jobs with unrestricted conditions to male workers and restricted (subordinate) jobs to female workers, where the only criterion was gender. Since this informal custom of allocation by gender was prohibited by the Equal Employment Law, managers made the courses (*sogo-shoku* and *ippan-shoku*) and allocated employees in, prima facie, a "legal" manner. For instance, if an applicant did not want overtime work (and most women did not), employers could legally allocate them to *ippan-shoku*.

The 1999 revision banned discrimination in employment and promotions, which seemed to close the main loopholes in the law. However, as was implied in the above data, women did not achieve equality in employment. One reason for the gap in employment by gender was discrimination based on the willingness to accept a job transfer (*tenkin*). That is, even after the 1999 revision, it was legal for employers to refuse women's applications for *sogo-shoku* if an applicant was reluctant to accept job transfers to distant places during her future career in that company. In short, direct discrimination has been prohibited by the 1999 revision, but indirect discrimination based on the willingness to accept one of the indeterminate features of men's working customs remained.

This indirect discrimination based on the refusal to relocate for a job was prohibited in the third major revision in 2007. Now, employers cannot reject women's application for *sogo-shoku* positions "without a rational reason." Employers can still reject a woman who is reluctant to accept a job transfer if the company has been conducting job relocations. As was shown previously, in most large companies, there are actual records of transfers to distant places.

To put it simply, the law prohibits gender discrimination only if an applicant is willing to accept the indeterminate features of work customs. Since a substantial number of women do not like the idea of being transferred to distant places, the proportion of female employment in *sogo-shoku* positions in large companies is still low.

The purpose of the Equal Employment Law is to introduce more women to the world of work by abolishing the apparent barrier between them and men. In that world, an employee never refuses job changes and transfers to distant places, and eventually accepts unlimited overtime work. He, as a *sogo-shoku* worker, cannot refuse them anyway because they are considered legal work orders, the refusal of which could lead to dismissal.

Now the most important point becomes clear. What has been consistently lacking in policy interventions to encourage women's economic activity is an attempt to change the masculine working customs to entice more women to join the core labor market. The Childcare Leave Act of 1992 and the expansion of day-care services based on the Angel-Plans were not intended to change the working customs, but to ease the burden of childcare for female workers. However, women, even after efforts to ease the burden of childcare, still have heavy responsibilities at home. Therefore, companies often put them on the "mommy track" with fewer duties and little possibility of promotion (Yu 2002). As Nakano observes, the true crisis for a working mother is not during the maternity leave period but after she returns to the workplace (Nakano 2014).

After all, for a person to make a full commitment to work, he or she has to be free from household responsibilities, and for a married worker to accept distant transfers, that worker must be the sole breadwinner. Otherwise, the spouse must quit working or change employers. It is very difficult for two *sogo-shoku* workers to get married and become a dual-earner couple. A male worker in the 1970s and 1980s was able to work without constraints because he had a housewife who provided full support at home. Similarly, a woman needs someone who supports her at home in order to work like a man.

The Equal Employment Law was destined to fail from the start because it was, throughout several revisions, meant to introduce women to men's working world. What is truly needed is to change Japanese working customs.

References

Abegglen, James C. 1958. *The Japanese factory*. Glencoe: The Free Press.
Brinton, Mary C. 2010. *Lost in transition: Youth, work, and instability in postindustrial Japan*. Cambridge University Press.
Doeringer, Peter B., and Michael J. Piore. 1971. *Internal labor markets and manpower analysis*. Lexington: Heath Lexington Books.
Fong, Eric, and Junya Tsutsui. 2015. The high cost of missing a boat under the Japanese recruitment practices: Timing of regular and non-regular employment after school completion in Japan. *Research in Social Stratification and Mobility* 42: 1–10.
Haitani, Kanji. 1978. Changing characteristics of the Japanese employment system. *Asian Survey* 18: 1029–1045.
Hamaguchi, Keiichiro. 2009. Atarashii Rodo Shakai [*A new labor society*], Iwanami (in Japanese).
Jacoby, Sanford. 1979. The origins of internal labor markets in Japan. *Industrial Relations* 18: 184–196.
Lechevalier, Sébastien. 2017. The "Re-segmentation" of the Japanese labour market. In *Social inequality in post-growth Japan: Transformation during economic and demographic stagnation*, ed. David Chiavacci, and Carola Hommerich, 57–72. Routledge.
Mouer, Ross, and Horosuke Kawanishi. 2005. *A sociology of work in Japan*. Cambridge: Cambridge University Press.
Nakano, Madoka. 2014. Ikukyusedai no Jirenma [*The dilemma of the maternity leave generation: Why has female empowerment failed?*] Kobunsha (in Japanese).
Nomura, Masami. 1998. Koyo Fuan [*Employment anxiety*]. Iwanami (in Japanese).
Taira, Koji. 1988. Economic development, labor markets, and industrial relations in Japan. In *The Cambridge history of Japan: Volume 6 the twentieth century*, ed. Peter Duus, 606–653. Cambridge University Press.
Yu, Wei-Hsin. 2002. Jobs for mothers: Married women's labor force reentry and part-time, temporary employment in Japan. *Sociological Forum* 17: 493–523.

Chapter 5
Work and Family in Japan from the Comparative Perspective

Abstract In this chapter, the characteristics of the Japanese-style life security system are explored and their implications for women's active labor force participation are discussed. In the context of the comparative welfare states theory, the Japanese welfare state is difficult to categorize based on the common framework used to classify Western capitalist states. The Japanese style of life security can be characterized by its unique employment security system and concomitant welfare provisions by family members, especially women. This regime has been consolidated by a conservative political movement since the late 1970s. Since the 1990s, the government has announced a series of political interventions to tackle the problem of the shrinking population. One of its goals was to increase the labor force by encouraging women to enter it. However, in order to introduce women to the working population, the Japanese style of employment security must be modified.

Keywords Japanese welfare state · Comparative welfare state theory · Employment security · Politics · Female labor force participation

5.1 Welfare Regime Typology and the Life Security System in Japan

Since the seminal work of Esping-Andersen, the welfare states theory has been one of the major frameworks for comparative study to explore the heterogeneity of social welfare among advanced capitalist societies. Arguments regarding the characteristics of Japanese society have also been affected by this framework of welfare states. Since the 1990s, copious literature and disputes have emerged surrounding the question: "What characterizes the Japanese welfare state?"

This question, which stems from the typology argument of welfare states by Esping-Andersen (Esping-Andersen 1990, 1999), does not have a direct relationship with the discussion about work and family issues that is developed here. Nonetheless, a comparative consideration between Western welfare and that of Japan provides certain important insights into the discussion. Esping-Andersen himself

Table 5.1 The welfare states typology by Esping-Andersen

	Liberal regime	Conservative regime	Social democratic regime
Model country	The United States	Germany	Sweden
Social expenditure	Small	Large	Large
De-commodification	Low	Medium	High
Stratification	Selective	Stratified	Universal

has recently contributed to family and gender equality issues (Esping-Andersen 2009; Esping-Andersen and Billari 2015). This indicates that those issues are an important point for understanding the contours and futures of capitalist countries.

Before discussing the Japanese-style welfare society, let us look at a brief overview of the welfare states typology by Esping-Andersen. The famous "three worlds of welfare capitalism" concept is illustrated in Table 5.1 (Esping-Andersen 1999). Two criteria are very important for characterizing welfare states. One is de-commodification, which refers to a situation in which a person can withdraw from the labor market without risking a negative impact on his well-being. The other is stratification, which refers to a situation in which access to welfare services is differentiated according to social class or occupational group.

Sweden is typical of the social democratic regime. The highly de-commodified and universal social security of this regime is usually made possible by taxation, not by a social insurance system. The government provides social services and benefits in a universal manner; they are not differentiated by social class or gender.

Germany is typical of the conservative regime. The social security system of this regime depends largely on social insurance schemes, and it is oftentimes segmented by occupational groups. The security function of this regime is multilayered. The minimum unit is the family. In the second layer, communities, churches, and occupational associations play a role. If those entities are not enough to provide for a person's well-being, public welfare is provided mainly by income transfers (Shizume and Kondo 2013, p. 8). The focus of the social security system in the conservative regime is the male breadwinner. The life security of family members is usually attained by securing the employment or income of male breadwinners.

Last, the United States is categorized as the typical liberal regime. Public social expenditures, whether for social services or for income transfers, are minimized. Therefore, the extent of de-commodification in this regime is quite low and the accessibility of social security plans is limited.

Esping-Andersen himself stated that the Japanese welfare system is a hybrid form of the liberal and conservative regimes (Esping-Andersen 1990). In Japan, the general level of public social spending and welfare generosity is rather low, which is an important feature of liberal regimes. However, two major types of social insurance schemes (public health care plans and pension plans) have been in place for nearly half a century. Social insurance schemes are built on a mixed base of both public spending and payments by occupational groups.

5.1 Welfare Regime Typology and the Life Security System in Japan

Researchers have made many attempts to categorize the Japan's welfare society, but most have not succeeded in providing a consistent view. As stated, the policy orientations toward social security by the Japanese government have been peripatetic and implemented in a makeshift manner (Goodman and Peng 1997). The Japanese system lacks a consistent framework and it has been quite difficult to put it in a meaningful category.

If we think beyond the regime categorization business, however, we can find rather consistent and comprehensible development of the welfare system in Japan. A consistent story can be built if we take the Japanese employment system, which was explained in a previous chapter, into consideration.

An important framework is provided by Miyamoto (2008) in this regard. Miyamoto proposes the term "life security" to refer to the basic framework a society provides to secure members' lives. Life security in a modern society is attained basically through social security and employment security. Social security provides life security for members through a series of public programs. By contrast, employment security, which means to secure members' lives via stable employment, is mainly provided by the private sector. Miyamoto's basic argument is that the main scheme of the Japanese welfare state depends on employment security rather than on the public framework.

This argument can be extended by considering the characteristics of the employment customs and the labor market in Japan, detailed in the previous chapter. Japanese private companies, especially large-scale ones, developed a unique system of labor force allocation. Even when the business was in a slump, a company could minimize the number of discharges by internal coordination of the labor force. A worker, in most cases, could expect that their status was secure. In exchange, they had to accept the possibility of a transfer to another type of job or to a distant place as well as the likelihood of chronic overtime.

The labor force adjustment in the internal labor market is only possible if an organization has a certain scale. For small- or medium-sized companies, it was much more difficult to execute the same kind of internal adjustments because most of them did not have as many departments or business locations as large-scale companies did. Therefore, in order to secure the employment of those working at small- and medium-sized companies, the Japanese government provided a variety of bail-out packages.

As stated in the previous chapter, the existence of small-sized family businesses contributed to absorbing the labor surplus during times of economic recession in Japan. Various types of regulations were implemented to protect family businesses from the invasion of large capital. A typical regulation was the "Large-Scale Retail Stores Law," which was meant to restrict the opening of large supermarkets in the vicinity of local shopping areas comprising small retail stores run by self-employed families. This law came into effect in 1974 and was abolished in 2000 in response to external pressure from the United States.

For small- and medium-sized companies, for which it was difficult to maintain an excess labor force within the organization, many public schemes were available. They included public loans at relatively low interest rates, public employment aids, and debt guarantees by public credit guarantee associations ("Shinyo-hosho-kyokai").[1] A relatively high level of spending for public works projects also helped to maintain employment for those working at small- and medium-sized companies.[2]

In sum, the core engine of Japanese welfare society, at least from the 1960s to 1980s, was employment security. For big companies, employment was secured by labor adjustments within each internal labor market. For medium- and small-sized companies, indirect employment protection measures by public programs have had a major role in securing employment.

In the previous chapter, it was argued that the system of internal labor adjustment worked against women's employment, since the nature of work was indeterminate in three ways (working time, job type, and working location). That the employment in small- or medium-sized firms is oftentimes supported by public employment protection programs may also have some impact on women's workforce participation. Because of public support programs, even a lame-duck company might be able to survive in an extremely competitive market. Those companies, unlike large-scale companies or small- and medium-sized companies in good standing, cannot provide decent work conditions, to say nothing of generous family-friendly programs for their employees. In short, working conditions in small- and medium-sized businesses are not likely to be suitable for women with child- and eldercare responsibilities for different reasons than those of large companies.

5.2 Politics of Work and Family

The Japanese style of employment security framework could not function without the other side of the welfare provisions. A male breadwinner, secured by the employment system, supported his family members through his income. On the other hand, family members, especially the wife, supported the male breadwinner by handling most of the housework and care work.

The Japanese-style of welfare system, put simply, was built on work organizations and family, both of which were private sector entities. This unique system developed during the era of high economic growth and matured in the 1980s. Direct political arrangements or interventions have been relatively low profile in the area of welfare provision.

Nonetheless, some political orientations did impact the formation of the Japanese-style welfare society. As described in Chap. 3, throughout the period of high economic growth and the subsequent period (up to the 1980s), tax and social insurance schemes gave advantages to male breadwinner households. These systems have been

---

[1] For details, see Kitayama and Joshita (2013, p. 340).
[2] Rates of spending for public works in Japan were approximately 5–6% as a percentage of the GDP from the 1970s to 1990s, which was relatively higher than the level in other advanced capitalist states such as the United States (around 4%) or Germany (2–3%).

5.2 Politics of Work and Family   49

maintained up to the present. There was an underlying political move that had an influence on the formation of the unique social system of Japan.

One of the major political factors in postwar Japan was its relationship with the United States. In particular, the politics surrounding the Japan–US Security Treaty produced a series of intense battles between the administrations of the time and the opposition parties and led to massive-scale civic protest campaigns. Partly with the intention to avert people's attention from this intense political situation, the leaders of Liberal Democratic Party (LDP) forced economic and welfare policies to the front burner in the 1960s. A typical case was the political strategy of Hayato Ikeda's administration. He proposed the famous "income-doubling plan" soon after he took office. This major shift in economic priorities was accompanied by the development of several important welfare programs. The National Pension System was instituted in 1960, and the National Health Insurance program followed the year after.

The emphasis on two sets of agendas, namely the economy and the welfare, continued until the early 1970s. Kakuei Tanaka's administration advocated the "first year of welfare society (Fukushi-Gannen)" in 1973, with the provision of generous welfare packages such as free medical care for the elderly. Public social spending increased by 29% from the previous year.

This basic trend of politics was forced to an end by the energy crisis in 1973. The basic orientation changed to the constraint or retrenchment of welfare provisions. However, the welfare retrenchment did not receive marked opposition. The reason was that employment security was relatively stable even in the 1980s. As stated earlier, the employment situation in Japan in the following period was not so bad compared to that of its Western counterparts. Some intellectuals started to assign positive evaluations to the Japanese society. One of the most marked cases was the monograph "Japan as Number One: Lessons for America" by the US sociologist Ezra Vogel, which was published in 1979.

In line with this political current, a conservative idea about the welfare society appeared within the ranks of the LDP. Under the Masayoshi Ohira administration, a research group under the LDP organization revealed the "Japanese-Style Welfare Society Plan" in 1979, and the discussions in the groups were published in a book of the same title in 1982.

This plan for the "Japanese-Style Welfare Society" had a distinct premise: it gave a clear negative judgement of the Swedish-style welfare state and put emphasis on self-reliance in welfare provisions. The authors of the book often used the phrase "the advanced nation's disease" to criticize generous public welfare provisions. A paragraph from the preface of the book said:

> It will become a danger if, by the abuse of welfare programs found in the so-called Swedish disease or British disease, people lose the morale to work, forget the spirit of self-reliance, and depend on public protections in every matter (The Liberal Democratic Party of Japan 1982, p. 16).

This political orientation, however, was not the way to a liberal regime (as in the United States) in Esping-Andersen's typology. It is indisputable that life security through private sector employment worked relatively well in the 1980s in Japan, which demotivated Japanese administrations from providing generous "de-commodification" programs. The same factor also worked to maintain the male breadwinner model, which had begun to fall out of favor in most Western societies.

A familialist tone[3] in the discussion of welfare at that time also gave indirect support to the "Japanese-Style Welfare Society Plan." In 1978, according to a White Paper from the Welfare Ministry, the high rate of elderly people who lived with their children's families in Japan was praised as a "hidden asset" of elderly welfare, since welfare provision for the elderly by family members (usually wives) could help the country save on public spending for elderly care.

Thus, the maturity of the Japanese welfare society in the 1980s was buttressed by the following factors: a relatively strong economy and stable employment, gender-based division of labor as a necessary result of Japanese employment customs, and the basic familialist orientation that worked to constrain public welfare provision.

5.3 A Possible Means of Encouraging Female Employment

The previous two sections in this chapter explain the background of the familialist regime of Japanese society from the perspective of the welfare states theory and politics. It becomes clear that the 1980s are the bifurcation point dividing societies: one with a relatively gender-neutral egalitarian orientation and Japanese society, which stills holds fast to a relatively strong gender-based division of labor. For some countries, economic hardships in the 1980s, especially high unemployment rates for men, were followed by an increase in dual-earner households. In Japan, because of the relative strength of men's employment and concomitant conservative policies, this shift in regime from the male breadwinner household to the dual-earner household did not see such distinct progress.

In this section, a possible means of fostering a dual-earner society in Japan is suggested. When we think about the basic design of our society, a "dual-earner" solution can be understood as a preferred alternative to the "male breadwinner" model, especially when considering the serious problems of low birthrates and an aging population. It is crucial for Japan to seek a way that does not force women to face a trade-off between having a successful career and motherhood. A massive need for eldercare will inevitably arise, and it is very important to ease the trade-off for women in order to maintain or increase the birthrate.

The first step to encourage a dual-earner society is to raise the marriage (or coupling) rate. As suggested in Chap. 2, most of the decline in fertility in Japan since the 1970s can be explained by the decrease in the marriage rate. Chapter 2 also suggested that the functional failure in the marriage market was caused by the increase

---

[3]"Familialist" here refers to an orientation that puts emphasis on the provision of welfare by family members instead of public organizations or private firms. This argument often idealizes the "good old family" where (at least according to the proponents' definition) family members, especially the wife, provide care for the elderly or for children.

5.3 A Possible Means of Encouraging Female Employment

Table 5.2 Political moves in the area of gender equality and aging population

1992	First introduction of the childcare leave act
1994	First "Angel Plan" to enlarge child day-care services
2003	Enactment of the "Basic Act for Measures to Cope with Society with Declining Birthrate"
2007	Pronouncement of the "Work-Life Balance Charter"
2015	Enactment of the "Act on Promotion of Women's Participation and Advancement in the Workplace"
2016	Pronouncement of the "Dynamic Engagement of All Citizens" plan

in women with high educational qualifications who hoped to "marry up," while the number of men with favorable status stagnated. This mismatch happened because the basic design of the country has not changed from the gender-divisional regime. This conservative gender regime is the result of unique conditions in employment and working systems (see Chap. 4) and a conservative political orientation (see the preceding sections in this chapter).

There are some movements to change this stagnant situation in terms of work and family in Japan. In the political context, the problem of the aging population has been an important item on the agenda since the 1990s (see Table 5.2 for a series of political events and movements). Along with it, the issue of gender inequality in employment has also made occasional appearances in the political arena. The second Abe administration has shared the same orientation since 2013.

To address the gender inequality problem, the Act on Promotion of Women's Participation and Advancement in the Workplace was enacted in 2015, which required large companies to make plans to promote women's activities, such as setting goals to increase the proportion of female managers in organizations. However, the motivation for increasing the female labor force seems to come less from the perspective of gender equality and more from the awareness of the labor force shortage as a result of the shrinking population. The Act on Promotion of Women's Participation was, in fact, promoted under the cabinet's slogan "The Dynamic Engagement of All Citizens." The implication of this slogan was that the solution to overcoming the problem of an aging population was to increase the potential labor force to include more women and the elderly. The rapid introduction of the new Immigration Control Act in 2018, which was enacted to increase acceptance of foreign workers, was also a part of this political drive.

What is lacking in this flow of political interventions is a move to bring substantive changes to the employment and working customs of Japan. The "Work-Style Reform" was an important measure on the agenda in the second Abe administration, and it resulted in the enactment of the Labor Reform Bill in 2018. It was certainly a groundbreaking law which, for the first time, introduced a ceiling for working hours. However, it still allows an average four hours of overtime work a day.

Long hours are not the only feature that prevents women's active participation in employment. As shown in Chap. 4, in order to promote the economic participation of a person with home responsibilities, the job should be relatively "restricted" in terms of time and location.

Introducing and increasing restricted jobs as a measure to encourage women to participate in the workforce, however, often encounters protests from labor groups. As has been previously explained, the system of the internal labor market can secure employment if it is possible to adjust the labor force by removing restrictions from the worker's hours and location. Therefore, employees of restricted jobs are more likely to be dismissed.

Employment security in Japan has been possible at least partly because of the unrestricted nature of employment, and not because of public programs for unemployment and job training. Therefore, putting emphasis on the restriction without consolidation of public support programs will inevitably lead to an unstable situation. This trade-off, however, is rarely discussed in the political context and media stories.

References

Esping-Andersen, Gosta. 1990. *The three worlds of welfare capitalism*. Cambridge: Polity Press.
Esping-Andersen, Gosta. 1999. *Social foundations of postindustrial economies*. Oxford: Oxford University Press.
Esping-Andersen, Gosta. 2009. *The incomplete revolution*. Polity Press.
Esping-Andersen, Gosta, and Francesco C. Billari. 2015. Re-theorizing family demographics. *Population and Development Review* 41: 1–31.
Goodman, Roger, and Ito Peng. 1997. The East Asian welfare states: Peripatetic learning, adaptive change, and nation-building. In *Welfare states in transition*, ed. Gosta Esping-Andersen, 192–224. Sage Publications.
Kitayama, Toshiya, and Kenichi Joshita. 2013. Nippon: Fukushi Kokka Hatten to Posuto Ruikei Ron [Japan: The development of welfare state and the post-typological theory]. In Hikaku Fukushi Kokka [*Comparative studies of welfare states*], ed. Masato Shizume and Masaki Kondo. Miverva (in Japanese).
Miyamoto, Taro. 2008. *Welfare politics: Life security and democracy in Japan*. Yuhikaku (in Japanese).
Shizume, Masato and Masaki Kondo. 2013. Fukushi Kokka wo Hikaku Suru Tameni [For a comparison of welfare states]. In Hikaku Fukushi Kokka [*Comparative studies of welfare states*], ed. Masato Shizume and Masaki Kondo. Miverva (in Japanese).
The Liberal Democratic Party of Japan. 1982. Nihongata Fukushi Shakai [*The concept of the Japanese welfare society*]. The LDP public relations (in Japanese).

Chapter 6
Japan's Changing Families and Future Agenda

Abstract In Japan, postwar reformation liberated families from the traditional patriarchy. However, this restructuring did not lead to gender egalitarianism in families. In part, this seemingly liberal change conformed to conservative ideals, in that it presupposed a family structure divided by gender. Households trended toward a gender-based division of labor, which simply represented a new type of male dominance. As a consequence of this change, academicians' focus shifted from the democratization of family life to the protection of women lacking economic independence. Japan's pursuit of gender equality is a work in progress. Meanwhile, an aging population is causing problems that cannot be remedied by gender equalization. To address the concerns of a society where single-person households are becoming ever more prevalent, a social security system must be built which can effectively support these individuals.

Keywords Patriarchy · Gender equalization · Aging population

6.1 The Departure from the Family Patriarchy

Things which are recognized as challenges in family life differ based on time period. What may be considered problematic in one era is often inapplicable, or even incomprehensive at other times. For this reason, it is difficult to understand family agendas using simple frameworks, such as the "conservatism versus liberalism" dichotomy.[1] For instance, conservatism and liberalism sometimes clash, and at other times conform, with each other regarding the propriety of government intervention in family formation. Moreover, the types of interventions which may be necessary is a continuing topic of discussion.

In this chapter, the changing forms and agendas of Japanese families are described. Based on this retrospective understanding, future possibilities are proposed for Japan's families.

---

[1] A trial for building a more sophisticated framework regarding family and long-term care policies can be found in Hieda (2012).

The first major agenda following World War II was breaking away from patriarchal family norms. Patriarchy in Japanese families was formally institutionalized by the Meiji Civil Code, implemented in 1898. The Code was informed by old family customs common among the warrior caste during the Tokugawa period. It established the incontestable authority of patriarchs, or householders. A male householder possessed the power to decide who was an official member of said household. That is, he had the right to incorporate a child conceived with his mistress as a new member of the family. The inclusion of a child born out of wedlock typically occurred when the householder and his lawful wife had no sons. Essentially, a lawful wife had no right to refuse her husband's decisions. The householder also had the right to decide where his children would live, and who they would marry. The family estate, or the set of a householder's status and rights, was to be ceded from the male householder to his lawful heir (in most cases the eldest son).

Actual application of these patriarchal norms depended on the circumstance at hand. Householders running a family business with important assets (such as a store or a factory) were more likely to exert greater control over other family members. For a self-employed family, the estate or assets were a necessary means of survival. A householder was in the position of managing the family business, giving him substantial dominion.

On the other hand, breadwinners in the new middle class (e.g., employed business persons or bureaucrats in public organizations) might have less authority than those running family businesses. Their power as householders was not backed by a family estate providing bread and butter for other family members. For a newly middle-class man, what mattered was the breadwinner's human capital; what children needed was a good education, not to inherit a family business.

Development of industrialization and urbanization in the Taisho era (from the 1910s to the early 1920s) provided women with many opportunities to earn income as clerks, telephone operators, teachers, etc. These jobs provided them with some independence from their families. On a societal level, this era represented a relatively democratic and liberal movement, retrospectively known as the "Taisho democracy." In the early 1920s, women fervently advocated for suffrage. Male householders' right to incorporate their mistresses' sons as household members (and legitimate inheritors) was challenged. The introduction of restrictions on this right was discussed, such that the lawful wife's agreement had to accompany any incorporation.

Although these movements elicited some excitement, male householders still held powerful sway over other family members. The Civil Code clearly prescribed the householder's superiority, while media and educational institutions also reflected these patriarchal norms. Such influences encouraged citizens' conformity. Further, liberal movements which flourished during the Taisho era were weakened, with authoritarian sensibilities prevailing as Japan transitioned into the war regime of the 1930s.

After defeat in the Pacific War led to the wartime government's collapse, the General Headquarters (GHQ) began establishing a series of campaigns. The basic intent of these initiatives was the abolishment of patriarchy, recognized by the GHQ as a source of aggressive authoritarianism. The Civil Code received a substantial revision, eliminating the power of householders. A majority of academicians in the fields of family law and sociology concurred with this move toward familial democracy. Legal scholar Takeyoshi Kawashima, one of the leading figures in postwar academia, argued that the Japanese people must discard old family customs in order to progress and become a democratic nation.

The departure from longstanding patriarchal customs was also brought about by changing economic structures as well as the revision of the legal system. As previously noted, the official sovereignty of householders had to be backed substantially by a family estate or business in order for them to exert their influence to its fullest potential. The popularization of employment, accompanied by the increase of large capital firms, dug away at traditional patriarchy's power source. Married couples were increasingly freed from the influence of their families of origin, as they were no longer affiliated with family businesses and could thus become economically independent.

6.2 Equal Rights Between Genders Without Equal Economic Opportunities

Increased employment (caused by industrialization and high economic growth in the 1960s and 1970s) did not free Japanese women from male dominance. A different type of male supremacy emerged in the wake of traditional patriarchy. During the period of high economic growth, men occupied the labor market (providing stable income), and "housewifization" proceeded. Husbands, with their ability to earn income, had relatively sturdier footing compared to wives. In other words, antiquated forms of patriarchal family dominance were replaced by a "modern type" of male hegemony, based upon the gendered division of labor.

As Emiko Ochiai described, married couples in the 1970s often lived harmoniously, presenting themselves as "husbands and wives like friends." Women's lack of work and career opportunities was not seen as a serious problem (Ochiai 1997). Young couples were relatively free from the power of their parents, enjoying an urban and consumer lifestyle. The flipside of this modern lifestyle was the economic dependence of wives on their husbands.

Shifts in mate selection provide compelling evidence of the evolution from the family patriarchy to more democratic, independent marriages. Such alterations reflect the transforming dynamic between parents and children. Figure 6.1 shows the trend in mate selection and the proportions of employment for males and females. The proportion of love marriages increased in concert with the bourgeoning employment rates for both genders.

Usually, transitions in mate selection are explained by the same factors which undermine the family patriarchy: a decrease in family businesses and an increase in employment. Increased employment levels influence mate selection in two main

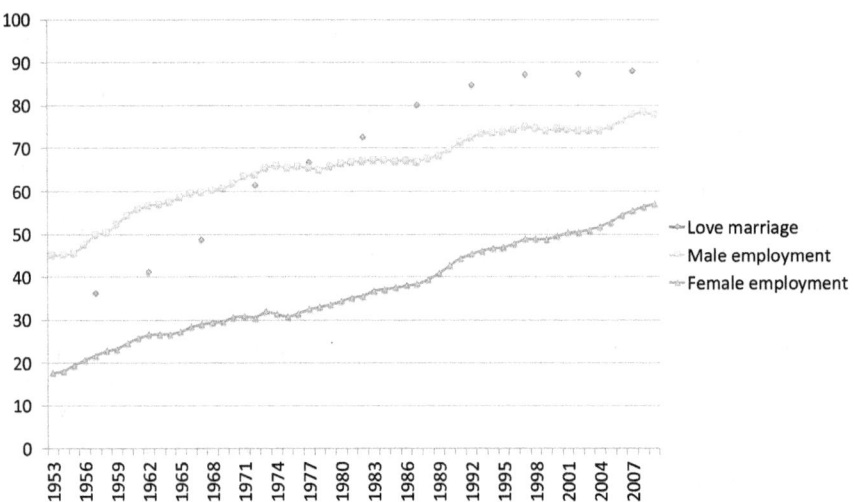

Fig. 6.1 Proportion of love marriages and employment. *Data* Information on the proportion of love marriages is from the National Fertility Survey in Japan. Statistics regarding proportions of employment based on percentages of workers are from the Labor Force Survey in Japan

ways. Firstly, the economic independence of children leads to autonomous decision-making, with mates selected by children themselves. Secondly, longer duration of education and increased employment outside the home boosts opportunities to meet members of the opposite sex (Thornton and Fricke 1987; Thornton et al. 1994).

Traditional mate selection, often called "arranged marriage" (as opposed to a love marriage), has two basic features. One is that the opportunity to meet a prospective partner is restricted and influenced by people besides the potential couple (typically, their parents). The other is that persons other than individuals hold authority over whether they will marry the person they are arranged to meet.

In Japan, the transition from outmoded patriarchal norms to more contemporary male-as-breadwinner households did not lead to a simple shift from arranged marriages to love marriages. This is typically represented by the Japanese custom of *Omiai*. Omiai is a type of arranged marriage, yet it differs from the typical arranged marriages described above. The difference is that in Omiai, a man and a woman usually make the decision for themselves. Parents or other matchmakers simply set up the opportunity to meet.[2] Tsutsui (2013) argues that more detailed categorization is necessary in order to grasp the modern intricacies of mate selection in East Asian society, including Japan.

Figure 6.2 shows the trends in four categories of mate selection, based on birth cohort. "Traditional arranged marriage" means that the initial meeting was orchestrated by parents or a matchmaker in the community, and parents also exerted substantial influence over marital decisions. The "introduced by parents" category refers to

---

[2] For a detailed analysis of contemporary Japanese mate selection, see Blood (1967) or Tokuhiro (2010).

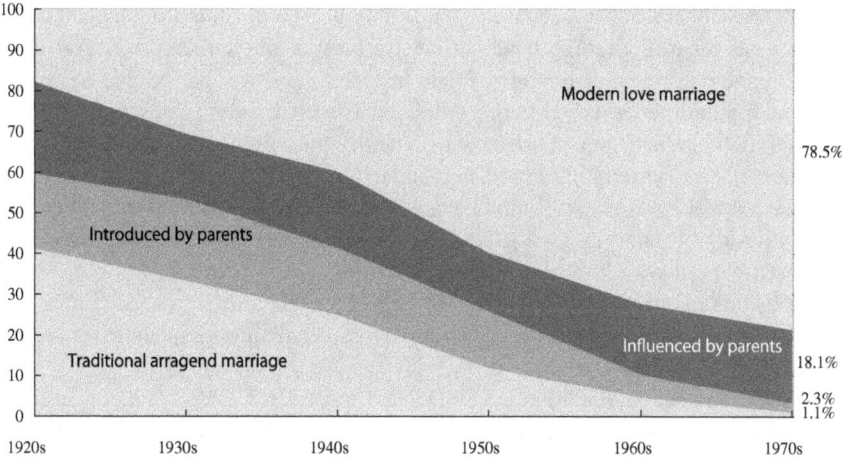

Fig. 6.2 Proportions of mate selection in four categories, by birth cohort. *Data* East Asian Social Survey 2006. For a detailed explanation of each category of mate selection, see Tsutsui (2013)

instances where the initial meeting was arranged, but parental influence on decision-making was weak. The "influenced by parents" category is the opposite of this: the initial meeting was instituted by the children themselves, but parental intervention concerning decision-making was rather strong. The last type, the "modern love marriage," is the polar opposite of the traditional arranged marriage. In such instances, a person meets his or her spouse of their own accord, and parental intervention is weak regarding decision-making.

As the figure indicates, the basic trend in mate selection in Japan is decreasing numbers of traditional arranged marriages and increasing numbers of modern love marriages. However, there have been a substantial number of marriages which fall into the "transitional" category of mate selection. Among them, the proportion of marriages where the couple initiated the preliminary meeting with their would-be spouse (but the decision was influenced by parents) was still over 18%. This was true even among the 1970s birth cohort. It is not shown in the chart, but the persistence of this type of mate selection was more prominent for females. That is, when deciding to marry someone she met by herself, a woman was more likely to receive parental intervention than a man.

This asymmetry can be understood by a renewed type of male dominance: the gender-based division of labor (Tsutsui 2013). Because the welfare of family members depends heavily on the earning power of the male breadwinner, parents of a daughter care more deeply about her choice of mate than parents of a son. As a result, parental intervention is much more pronounced regarding a daughter's choice of a prospective mate.

In short, couples from the 1960s to the 1980s were liberated from the obsolescent patriarchy, yet retained male dominance (as most households were reliant upon a male breadwinner). Partly because of this ambiguity, contrasting liberal and conservative ideas regarding family have not always been a simple dichotomy. As stated, the paramount concern of liberal scholars in Japan's postwar period was to remove political regulations based on family-related patriarchal codes. Conservative politicians argued against the total disposal of family patriarchy, as established by the previous (outdated) version of the Civil Code.

The task of liberal groups in the next generation (namely, during the era of gendered division of labor; i.e., from the 1960s to 1980s) was to protect women's lives. In those times, it was difficult for a woman to obtain a job which would provide a stable income. Consequently, family law scholars argued that protective measures were necessary, especially for women who divorced and thus lost their main income source.

The basic idea contained in the Civil Code (revised in 1948) is that concerning a husband and wife's marital property, each has separate ownership of their valuables; there is no legal prescription for co-ownership. However, in essence, the court admits the contribution of housewives to their husbands' earnings. When a divorce occurs, a settlement is made which halves the property, regardless of a bank account's holder. Most liberal legal scholars support this theory, emphasizing the value of domestic support by women.[3]

6.3 Declining Family Formations

The postwar idea of family democratization (i.e., liberation from the patriarchal influence of families of origin) and the subsequent notion of protecting women lacking opportunities to earn income were both compatible with the gender-divided system. Thus, in a manner, these two liberal concepts ("democracy" and the "protection of the weak") conformed to the conservative ideal of family by embodying the "male breadwinner and female homemaker" model.

In previous chapters, Japan's persistent gender division of work and family spheres was explained by the Japanese-style prioritization of life security: i.e., its unique employment stability for men, and the provision of care by family members (especially women). It was further argued that this system has been bolstered by the conservative political orientation emphasized since the late 1970s. Additionally, for the aforementioned reasons, pressure to increase government expenditures for family support has been weak, even from liberal sources.

As a reflection of these factors, civic spending on Japan's families has remained at a low level. Figure 6.3 shows both public social spending, and public family spending as a percentage of OECD countries' GDP. Among countries with the same level of public social spending as that of Japan, Japan ranks in the lowest group in terms of public family spending.

---

[3]This is sometimes referred to as the logic of "naijo-no-ko," meaning support given by housewives to husbands by work accomplished inside the home.

6.3 Declining Family Formations

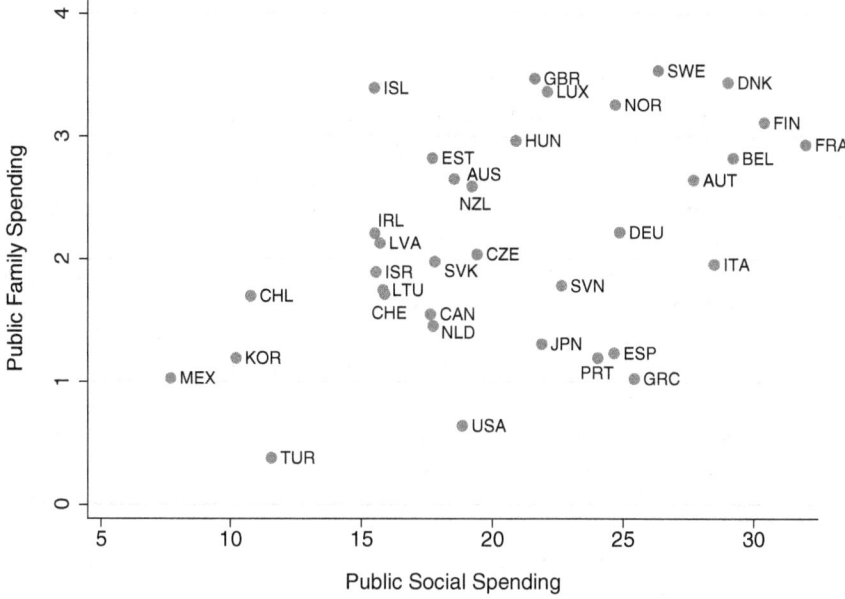

Fig. 6.3 Public social spending and public family spending in OECD countries for 2015. *Data* OECD, Social spending indicator. https://doi.org/10.1787/7497563b-en (Accessed 31 March 2019)

Figure 6.4 compares the trend of Japan's public family spending to the OECD average since 1980. It is easily recognizable that public support for family life in Japan has never been higher than the OECD average.

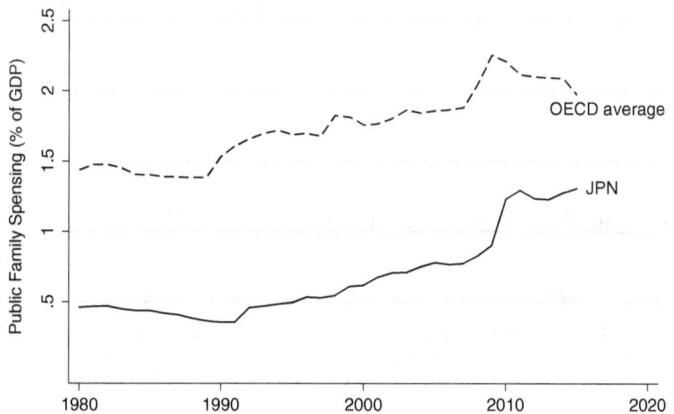

Fig. 6.4 Average Public family spending in Japan versus OECD countries (1980–2015). *Data* OECD (2019), Family benefits public spending (indicator). https://doi.org/10.1787/8e8b3273-en (Accessed 15 April 2019)

The essentially conservative nature of Japan's government was not expressly articulated as a manifest political program intended to intercede in family life. The major exception during the postwar period was an intervention in reproductive behavior via a public campaign on family planning. This initiative began with the implementation of the Eugenic Protection Law. As discussed in Chap. 3, a second exception promoted the male-as-breadwinner model through revisions of tax and social insurance schemes. Beginning in the 1990s (after a long period of almost no manifest family support policy), administrations suddenly began providing a series of family support packages. However, these were merely cursory responses to 1990s "1.57 shock" (see Chap. 2 in this volume), evoked by a release of the 1989 birthrate.

The increase in family spending since 2010 is mainly due to basic GDP growth trends among OECD countries. However, at least in part, it reflected the era's more liberal political orientation. Following the 2009 national election, the Democratic Party of Japan's (DPJ) Hatoyama administration took control of the government. Previously, Japan was led by the more conservative Liberal Democratic Party (LDP). The DPJ introduced a child allowance program containing far more generous funding than previous, similar initiatives.

The LDP regained power in the 2012 national election, but a series of programs intended to increase Japan's birth rate continues. Even though the 2nd Abe cabinet was basically conservative, it recognized that the aging population was one of the biggest challenges in Japan. Based on awareness of this crisis, spending for public childcare services has gradually increased.

As demonstrated in previous chapters, it is difficult to say whether the program package to increase birthrates has been successful. The primary reason for this uncertainty is that the main measure of birthrate increase has been the growing need for childcare support. However, it was off-target. Over 90% of the decline in birthrates since the 1970s can be explained by declining marriage rates (2017 Declining Birthrate White Paper), not by the change in birthrate for married couples.

The marriage rate continues to decrease. Partner mismatch (the main factor in the declining marriage rate) is caused by women's preference for marrying up; a rational choice in a society with gendered division of labor.

6.4 Aging and the Limits of Gendered Families

In this volume, it has been argued that concerted efforts to foster a dual-earner society are important steps in increasing marriage and birth rates. The most vital concern here is gender egalitarianism. Liberation from the gendered regime is still a crucial social task for Japan.

However, it must be noted forthwith that gender equality and the shift to a dual-earner society cannot address major, current problems caused by an aging population and declining marriage rate. A dual-earner, gender equal society will work, provided most people get married. For those in single-person households (i.e., individuals without partners), sharing income and household tasks is impossible.

Of course, in the long term, the dual-earner strategy will help with family formation and easing the problems of aging and low birthrates. However, it is also true that these strategies do not ameliorate today's problems of aging and a low marriage rate. According to the 2015 census, the proportion of households including a married couple was less than half (47.0%). The proportion of single-person households was 34.6%, a figure which has increased by 9.7% in the last 5 years. Among these single-person households, the number with individuals aged 65 years or older have increased by 23.7% (1.6 million) over the last 5 years.

Social security systems assuming households comprised of couples are losing their effectiveness. For a person living in a single-person household, support from other family members is not available. The importance of (and need for) public assistance is increasing.

Esping-Andersen argued that the movement toward a gender egalitarian system was an "incomplete revolution" (Esping-Andersen 2009). In Japan, and perhaps in several East Asian societies, the problem lies not only in the fact that the revolution is far from "complete." Perhaps the greatest concern is that the problems these nations face cannot be addressed merely by the achievement of a gender equal society.

References

Blood, Robert. O. 1967. *Arranged match and love marriage: A Tokyo-Detroit comparison*. New York: Free Press.
Esping-Andersen, G. 2009. *The incomplete revolution*. Polity Press.
Hieda, Takeshi. 2012. *Political institutions and elderly care policy: Comparative politics of long-term care in advanced democracies*. Palgrave Macmillan.
Ochiai, Emiko. 1997. *The Japanese family in transition: A sociological analysis of family change in postwar Japan*. LTCB International Library Foundation.
Thornton, Arland, Jui-Shan Chang, and Hui-Sheng Lin. 1994. From arranged marriage toward love match. In *Social change and the family in Taiwan*, ed. Arland Thornton and Hui-Sheng Lin, 148–177. Chicago: The University of Chicago Press.
Thornton, Arland, and Thomas E. Fricke. 1987. Social change and the family: Comparative perspectives from the West, China, and South Asia. *Sociological Forum* 2: 746–779.
Tokuhiro, Yoko. 2010. *Marriage in contemporary Japan*. New York: Routledge.
Tsutsui, Junya. 2013. The transitional phase of mate selection in East Asian countries. *International Sociology* 28: 257–276.

GPSR Compliance

The European Union's (EU) General Product Safety Regulation (GPSR) is a set of rules that requires consumer products to be safe and our obligations to ensure this.

If you have any concerns about our products, you can contact us on

ProductSafety@springernature.com

In case Publisher is established outside the EU, the EU authorized representative is:

Springer Nature Customer Service Center GmbH
Europaplatz 3
69115 Heidelberg, Germany